Strategies for Teaching
the Composition Process

Strategies for Teaching the Composition Process

Carl Koch, F.S.C.
Bergan High School

James M. Brazil
Community College of Baltimore

National Council of Teachers of English
1111 Kenyon Road, Urbana, Illinois 61801

Grateful acknowledgment is made for permission to reprint the following material. An excerpt from "Letters Home" by Thomas E. Kingsley which appeared in the June 1974 issue of *Harper's* magazine, by permission of Mrs. Fred Kingsley. "Women in TV-Land: You've Got a Long Way to Go, Baby" by Norman Mark, which first appeared in the May 1974 Chicago *Daily News* Panorama section. Copyright © 1974 by the Chicago *Daily News*. Reprinted by permission.

Staff Editor: William Ellet

Book Design: Tom Kovacs

NCTE Stock Number 47518

Copyright © 1978 by the National Council of Teachers of English. All rights reserved. Printed in the United States of America.

Library of Congress Cataloging in Publication Data

Koch, Carl, 1945–
    Strategies for teaching the composition process.

    1.   English language—Composition and exercises—Study and teaching.   2.   English language—Rhetoric—Study and teaching.   I.   Brazil, James M., 1941–joint author.   II.   Title.
PE1404.K6   808'.042'07   77-26325
ISBN 0-8141-4751-8

Contents

Acknowledgments

We wish first to thank Kathy Eisele, Delta College; Mary Dean, Shelby State Community College; and Jim Merlihan, Community College of Baltimore, for the valuable strategies they contributed to this book.

We would also like to thank the following individuals who have given us the benefit of sound advice and much needed support: Alberta Goodman, Miami-Dade Community College; Tim Davies, Polk Community College and former Director of the Doctor of Arts program at the University of Michigan; and Jay Robinson, Richard Bailey, Bernard Van't Hul, Alan Howes, and our other friends from the University of Michigan Doctor of Arts program. Finally, we thank our students, who have both taught and inspired us.

Introduction

Practical, involving, student-centered, simply implemented: these are a few of the attributes we think apply to the strategies described in this book. This is not a textbook; it is a book of immediately useable exercises, unencumbered by lengthy discussions of theory, for high school, community college, college, and university composition teachers. Theory is of course important in teaching because it is the indispensable ground for what one teaches and how one teaches. Our purpose, however, is to provide a resource book of strategies for the composition classroom that makes use of, but does not describe in detail, generally accepted research in composition. These strategies are designed to augment, not replace, the composition teacher's usual approach, and they need not be used in the order in which they are presented here. Since between the two of us we have taught all grades from junior high school to the senior year in college, we know that teachers must construct their courses according to their own goals and objectives. Therefore, strategies are to be selected to fit individual class needs. We have used these strategies successfully and we are certain that others can, too.

One of the basic premises from which we constructed these strategies is that students have a wealth of resources that they can tap for their writing. Research shows that students have tremendous potential for language acquisition, and classroom teachers know from their own experience that students have tremendous potential for language learning and use. Each student has opinions, insights, and experiences about which to write. How many times have teachers heard students tell lengthy, descriptive stories outside the classroom? Yet, these same stories rarely seem to appear in essays, either as narratives or as examples in expository writing. Why? Very often, teachers just don't know how to help students use their full range of language, ideas, and experiences. These strategies should aid the instructor in helping his or her students to use all of their resources.

Another reason that teachers do not very often get students to fully use their experiences and language in writing is that students feel uncomfortable doing so in class. The sources for this discomfort are many, and to account for all of them in this short introduction would do an injustice to their complexity; but it is clear that the school setting itself can be disconcerting, especially where emphasis is placed on competition among students. Another source of worry for student writers is that many times they perceive that their experiences are not acceptable to the teacher as subject material. Evidence for this is that students are often given topics about which they know little and are seldom given ways of gathering ideas about a topic. Just as important, students, especially nonstandard dialect speakers, are made to feel inadequate about their language. Either by comments written on their essays or corrections made of oral expressions, students are made to feel inferior about their ability to make language. Consequently, helping students feel comfortable about expressing themselves is as important as getting them in touch with what they know. Thus, besides building writing skills, each strategy in this book builds the class "comfort level." Obviously, a linguistically insecure person is not going to be a very effective writer. Confidence and skill develop together.

A rather different source of students' insecurity about writing is that they are often told to match their compositions with those of professionals. We have avoided the model and exercise approach here. We have found that in modeling their writing after a professional, students become imitators, not creators. In addition to feeling insecure about comparing their work to professionals, students usually have not developed ways of finding their own topics and of ordering their own ideas and experiences into communicable form.

Instead of using models, our strategies help students learn a compositional process; if one is skillful in teaching the process, the product will be acceptable. Our strategies help make writing essays a conscious process. By teaching students to consciously follow a process of writing, teachers can free them from slavishly imitating models. For instance, one of the strategies helps students to find their own topics. By learning how to do this, a student has learned a skill that is a prerequisite to becoming an independent, competent writer. The compositional process upon which our strategies are based is not original with us. A knowledge of Aristotelian rhetoric shows one that. However, our outline of the process (see chart) is a clear and succinct description of how most people go about writing.

While our outline is necessarily linear, the writing process is not; thus, some of the steps overlap chronologically. Also, this description

Stages of the Composition Process

Prewriting

1. **Experiencing**

   Our response to someone or something leading to a desire to communicate, e.g., wanting to write a letter to the editor after reading an editorial with which one disagrees.

2. **Discovering**

   Identifying a topic and an audience. (Often what moves one to write is an audience.)

3. **Making Formal Choices**

   Selecting a form for the essay—narrative, opinion, description, etc.—and a form of organization.

Writing

4. **Forming**

   Arranging essay materials in line with choices in step three, e.g., in a narrative, writing in chronological order; or, in an opinion essay, writing a clear thesis statement to begin the essay.

5. **Making Language Choices**

   Selecting language appropriate to one's purpose and audience, e.g., deciding between formal or informal wording, selecting adjectives, etc.

6. **Languaging**

   The process of carrying out the language choices, e.g., if one is writing a formal analysis, using language that is factual and exact.

Postwriting

7. **Criticizing**

   Evaluation of the essay to determine if it reflects the choices made earlier in the composition process, e.g., Does my opinion essay have a clear thesis statement? Did I describe my examples well enough? Will my audience understand the words I used?

8. **Proofreading**

   How does the essay meet the external standards of one's audience: form, punctuation, neatness, spelling, etc.?

of the writing process places proofreading in its proper position—last. After students have developed prewriting and writing skills, they can learn more about proofing.

The introductions to the sections of the book describe each step in the composition process more fully; following the explanations are strategies to help students master that part of the process. For example, following the explanation of prewriting are strategies for finding topics for essays, defining an audience, and choosing a method of development for essays.

If instructors used only this book for their classes, they would have enough activities to teach the entire compositional process. However, these exercises can be easily combined with material of one's own design. Each time we have used one of the strategies, we have altered it to fit the needs of that particular class at that specific time.

One of the strengths of these strategies is that they all require a great deal of student participation. Many of them are flexible enough to be used as activities for individuals, small groups, or the whole class. Since many teachers have had little if any training in directing small groups, we have given explicit procedures for the strategies to maximize their usefulness. Once teachers have directed a few activities, they will use and adapt them confidently. We expect that after using this process-oriented approach, teachers will also construct their own strategies.

As is suggested in many of the strategies, an effective way of increasing the involvement of students in the activities is for the instructor to participate. We have enjoyed sharing our ideas, experiences, and writing with our students. By doing this we have not only set many of them at ease, but have also stimulated them to try harder in their own work.

We have included two appendixes suggesting ways of evaluating student writing. For many composition teachers the distasteful part of teaching composition comes when they must write a response to an essay by a struggling student. Most English teachers have never been instructed how to do this in a constructive way. Too often they simply red-mark surface errors, as if their only job were proofreading. In the appendixes we point out ways of making constructive evaluative remarks about student writing so that students can build on their competencies. Of particular concern is how evaluations can help students with matters of form. Judging from our experiences, the suggestions that we make here work. That is, they encourage students to continually improve their essays without damaging their self-confidence.

Like much material aimed at improving classroom teaching methods, the strategies in this book occasionally involve the reproduction of previously published work. It goes without saying that we are not encouraging the copying of materials that exceeds the standards of fair use as defined in the Copyright Act of 1976. It is not our intention to give users of our book advice on the provisions of the act, but we recommend a statement by Robert F. Hogan, NCTE executive secretary, in the December 1976 issues of *English Journal* and *College English* as a useful summary of fair use as it applies to teachers.

The exercises that follow are not finished strategies because teachers will use them to develop better ways of teaching composition, but they are worthwhile as an immediate aid and a sound beginning. Teaching composition is an important endeavor. When we do it well—when a formerly incoherent student writer produces a full-blown, vivid paragraph or when a bright, motivated freshman turns in an incisive, well-developed essay—we feel real joy. These strategies have worked to bring a sense of confidence, and sometimes joy, both to us and to our students.

The Comfort Zone

Most English teachers have heard one of their students complain, "I don't know what to write!" It is a common occurrence, one that suggests both a profound insecurity about the act of writing on the part of students and a need for reassessing compositional goals and objectives on the part of English teachers. Since there is nothing inherently frightening about the act of writing—or at least nothing more than is felt in other common human acts—the fear must come from somewhere *outside* the writing act.

We suspect that "somewhere" is too often the composition classroom itself. For the greater part of their academic lives, linguistically insecure students have learned how poorly they write, how little they know about writing, and what pure drudgery a writing assignment can be. The almost automatic response—"I don't know what to write"—is a defense mechanism; after all, it is easier to admit your ignorance than to commit yourself to paper, exposing once more your fragile, tentative writing abilities to the merciless red pen.

Combating and alleviating this fear of writing should be primary goals for the composition instructor, regardless of the grade level he or she teaches. Whether it be a junior high English class or a freshman composition class at a major university, one of the first classroom goals for the teacher should be to create a "comfort zone" for his or her students, an environment that reduces threat, alleviates fear, and motivates students to become willing, even enthusiastic, participants in their own writing development.

Motivation is the key to learning. If students are not motivated to learn something, they will not do so, and education then becomes an empty, ludicrous game—a game where students are the real losers. Establishing an environment that encourages learning and motivates students to want more learning is a necessary priority for all classrooms, but it is especially important to the composition class, which inherits so many negative feelings from students' pasts.

No formulas or cure-alls exist for reducing fear, establishing a learning environment, and motivating students, but the instructor is certainly critical to accomplishing any of these in the classroom.

Teaching strategy and classroom structure are always modified by the personality and teaching skills of the instructor to produce a unique learning environment that can never be exactly duplicated by anyone else. The ideal personality for teaching composition, we feel, is one that encourages questioning and participation, that is genuinely warm and supportive (without being false or sentimental), and that encourages and motivates students to write more and write better. It is an ideal which leaves most of us lacking in some way, but that fact should not deter the teacher from trying to improve the way the classroom is run.

The first few weeks of a composition course are crucial to the success of the course: if the comfort zone is not established early, if the students are not motivated to think about language and to want to write better, and if student fear of writing and the composition classroom is not reduced at this early stage, then what happens afterwards may be futile and self-defeating.

The strategies that follow are designed for use in the early part of a composition course. They all have the same educational goals: to encourage students to think and talk about language, to convince students that they tacitly know a great deal about language and writing, and to establish an open, nonthreatening environment that encourages students to become active participants in their own learning.

1. The Name Game: Breaking the Ice

Group size: Entire class in large-group discussion circle.
Time required: Approximately forty-five minutes, depending on class size.
Materials: None.

Goals

A. To create an informal, relaxed classroom environment during the first or second class meeting.
B. To help everyone learn each other's name in the space of one class period.
C. To establish an atmosphere for later small-group exercises, such as peer essay sharing or small-group brainstorming sessions.

Process

A. The instructor briefly discusses the goals of the activity.
B. The instructor tells students to take one or two minutes to think of what name they want to be called during the rest of the semester and *two reasons* why they like that name.
C. The instructor asks for a volunteer to begin the exercise before giving the rest of the instructions for the game.
D. After someone volunteers to begin, the instructor explains that the process will move in a clockwise direction from that volunteer. Once the volunteer has given his or her name and two reasons for liking that name, the next person must repeat the preceding person's name and the two reasons before giving his or her name and reasons. The next student must also start with the volunteer, giving names and reasons for the first two students before stating his or her own name and reasons. In other words, the game gets progressively harder as it continues, since each student must start at the beginning. The instructor, of course, is a participant in the game and follows the rules when his or her turn comes. Students should be encouraged to relax and enjoy the process; if a participant has trouble remembering some names or reasons, other members should be encouraged to help out.
E. Once the game is finished, the instructor should inform the class that the reasons are no longer important, but that they should try to remember the names of their classmates and instructor.

Variations

A. To save time, only one reason can be given by each participant or no reason at all.
B. Students might have a short free-writing period in which to jot down reactions to the exercise.
C. Instead of reasons for names, participants might give their names and the animal they most admire or would like to be.
D. Students may be asked to write a short, spontaneous character description of the person who made the strongest impression on them. To be consistent with the goals of this strategy, these papers should be nongraded, but the teacher should respond to them in some fashion.

2. Student as Teacher: Perceiving Writing Priorities

Group size: The class should be broken into small groups of four to six members by any method the instructor chooses.
Time required: Fifty minutes to one hour. Twenty-five to thirty minutes in a large discussion group.
Materials: Copies of writing by unsophisticated writers. (Some examples are included at the end of this strategy.) Notepaper for each group.

Goals

A. To help students perceive writing priorities.
B. To encourage student thinking and discussions of language matters.
C. To encourage class participation.

Process

A. The instructor briefly discusses the goals of the activity and explains the general age and grade level of the people who wrote the material to be handed out.
B. The instructor explains that the students are to pretend that they are composition teachers and these writers are their students.
C. The instructor explains that each small group should read and discuss each writing before coming to a consensus on a list of three to five priorities they would follow to help that student develop into a better writer.
D. One student in each small group should act as a reporter to record the list of priorities and any dissenting opinions.
E. Each small group reports its list of priorities to the class. The instructor or a student volunteer can write the lists on the board.
F. The entire class constructs a "master" list of priorities for each writing, although complete agreement on the list is not necessary.
G. The instructor asks the students if the same priorities hold true for their *own* writing development and leads the ensuing discussion.

Variations

A. As an assignment, the instructor can have students write a list of priorities for their own writing development.

B. The instructor could substitute essays of his or her choice for the small-group discussion.
C. The priorities can be typed up and distributed to class members as a checklist for the analysis of their own papers.
D. The reporters could form a small group in the middle of the class to arrive at a consensus on priorities with the teacher. An open chair may be introduced into this small group so that any student not in it *could* contribute. Later, the class may be asked to give feedback to the inner group about how they functioned as a group.

Sample Essays

The following essays may be used for the small-group discussions described in this strategy.* The first was written by a seven year old on his first day in second grade; the second by a twenty-year-old community college student on her first day in an English class; and the third by a thirty-two-year-old community college student, also on his first day in an English class.

What I Did this Summer, 1974

I what [went] to Clifton Forgr [Forge] I what to vit [visit] my frib [friend] I spen [spent] the noit [night] afr ot [over at] my frib [friend's] We did fumny [funny] stuf.

[Essay untitled]

It was some experience when I first rode a subway train. I had never seen nothing that would go so fast. I go so fast I can't see the interest thing thats in the city. When it went under the tunnel it go dark quickly.

The train rocked from one side to the other. It went really fast to me. I saw new people get on the train before the door close.

The first car in front stop. Then the rest of the cars stopped. I seem to me that the cars in back are going to crash and I get very scared. The people in the train are so crowd. I saw there was a hole between the train track and the station. I had to be careful not to step in the hole.

One of the best experience I had was riding on a subway train in the big city. Watching people walking up and down the street. So many big building and apartment houses.

I always wanted to become a top mechanic

I always wanted to become a top mechanic. When I was seven years old I watched cars an often wondered what made them

---
*The student writing included in this and other strategies has not been edited or corrected.

run. So at thtat time I stared bying books and other material on cars and there parts, to try and fine out what made them run. By the time I was old enough to get a drivers license, I knew a great deal about cars. By the time I reached my senior year in school, I had made up my mine that I wanted to become the best mechanic in this country. After school, I went on to mechanic school for two years, and after that, got a job as a mechanic for Ford Motor Company. After being there for a few years, I became the top mechanic, and was named mechanic of the year for Ford Motor Company.

3. Evaluating Essays

Group size: Class should be split up into groups of around five members each.

Time required: Fifty minutes if the evaluating is done outside of class time; add about twenty minutes if the reading of essays is to be done in class.

Materials: Copies of the essays to be evaluated for each student.

Goals

A. To have students evaluate writing and establish criteria for good writing.
B. To help students understand their innate ability to recognize good writing.
C. To facilitate the working together of class members so that they become better acquainted.
D. (Optional) To engage students in grading essays and establishing criteria for grades.
E. (Optional) To have students experience a consensus decision-making situation.

Process

A. Discuss the goals of the exercise with the class.
B. Pass out three essays to be evaluated. (Four sample essays are included at the end of this strategy.)
C. Instruct the students to read carefully each essay you have chosen and, while they are reading the essay, to write comments about it. They are to tell why and how the paper represents good and/or bad writing.
D. (Optional) You may tell them to assign the paper a grade.
E. Split them into the small groups.
F. For the following part, which takes about twenty-five minutes, give them these instructions: "You have all evaluated three essays. Now, you should have a person in your group who will report the results of your discussion to the whole class. Each member of your group should read to the group his or her evaluation of the first essay. After all members have read their evaluations, the group should select the comments most often mentioned. These comments should be taken down by the person recording. Continue to discuss the group's evaluation of the essay until all commonly agreed upon critical remarks are

part of your report. Repeat the process on essay two and essay three. Remember you should take only about twenty-five minutes for this."

G. When all groups are finished, each reporter should give the evaluation of his or her group. Discuss each group's evaluation of essay one before hearing evaluations of essay two.

H. The teacher or a student may write a summary evaluation on the board.

I. When all of the evaluations are completed, the class should be able to discuss the probable similarities of the groups' evaluations.

J. The teacher may wish to point out, in summary, that all persons have an inherent capacity for language learning and that most of us know when a piece of writing communicates or does not. Finally, point out that the criteria for a good essay can indeed be established.

K. Either with the whole class or in small groups, you may wish to decide on a list of criteria for a good essay, moving from most important to least important.

Variations

A. If class members are writing journals or are doing free writing, this exercise often stirs some interesting student reflections on writing.

B. You may wish to split up the groups according to the grades given each essay. For example, on essay one, have all those who gave it an A in one group, those who gave it a B or C in another group, and so on. (Usually, widespread disagreement is uncommon.)

C. If you grade essays, you might share with the students the priority listing of criteria for your own evaluation of their papers.

D. You may want to duplicate the list of criteria and distribute it to your students, suggesting that they check their writing using the criteria before turning in assignments.

E. Very often students find many problems in the sample essays and very few good points. You might instruct them to mark only the positive elements of the samples. This would be a good way of showing that there is something worthwhile in just about every essay.

F. If you had the students take notes about the discussion on criteria, they might write an essay about their opinions on the subject, using the reasons given in class as supporting arguments for their thesis.

Sample Essays

The following may be used for writing evaluation. Obviously, they may not fit your needs, so, if available, use essays by former students of yours. The first two essays were written by high school seniors and the second pair by college freshmen.

Law and Order

People talk of law, order and justice, but many people do not realize that there is no law and order nor justice among nations of man. They are lawless including the United States our country in its external relations with other nations. They spend millions of dollars building up unnessary arnments and armed forces. If this is allowed to continue our fate has been already decided. For inevitable, the preparations for war will led to war accidentally or intentionally.

The people of the world must convinse there leaders that the way to peace is not through armed conflict between nations. Militarism and nationalism must give way to the common good of all mankind. There are urgent world problems both in the developed and developing nations that it is imperative that the state of total and complete disarmment whereas all nations mutal agree to terms discerming and disbanning there armies and that there weapons turned into instruments of peace and prosperity.

[Essay untitled]

I decided to go to church this Sunday, I wasn't too tired, I hadn't been here in a long time, so I came this Sunday. I can't hardly stand going to church anymore I'm usually too tired from Saturday night but I go once in awhile to make an appearance and to look at the pretty girls. The pretty girls I think go to show off their bodies in the shortest and prettiest dresses I've ever seen. I wonder if they know that they keep poor bastards like me from falling asleep. The older people so pomp and pious deeping track of how much him and her put in the collection box. They also stare at you if you happen to have wore jeans that morning or if you left during communion. There are a couple of reasons why I don't like church anymore, it's not because I'm tired, because I'm tired most of the time. I went every school day from fourth to eighth grade with nuns watching and making sure you went in. I swear I knew every word and move the priest did up there. Also I don't feel when I go to church that this is my mass, it seems like older peoples mass. I want the mass in a language I can understand. Church also seems like a social event anymore, where people dress up in best clothes make a grand appearence at church and talk about whom or whatever you want after church. I think of what goes on in these people's minds at church. The little baby is hungry and doesn't know what the hell is going on and will be glad when this thing is over so he can eat. Little Billy sees Johny and has to catch him after church to see if he wants to play football. Dave and Roger and Greg are playing and probably Bill will play who else can I get to play? Older Ted is thinking about Doris two pews ahead in that red miniskirt, he just has to talk to her after church. Mom is wondering if she should cook breakfast or have everybody eat coffee and donuts in the school hall. Dad is thinking about the afternoon football game and can't wait till he gets home and hopes he hasn't missed any of it. Grandpa and Grandma I think are pretty sincere, they know that their time is near and I really think there sincere. So if it stays the same I will probably be sincere when I hit about 60 or 70. But I don't think these few Masses will make up for everything, and maybe I won't live till 60, then what will I do.

Amnesty to All

For at least the past ten years the United States has been involved in a war over in Vietnam. During these years men were drafted or forced to fight for freedom, even though it was so far away and not their home which was in danger. But in every human there is a need for survival and a fear of death. Therefore out of this feeling came people called "draft-doggers." These are people who do not believe that anything can be settled by killing and refuse to do so. I do not think that anything can be settled by killing and refuse to do so. I do not think that anyone could condemn a person for such actions. As I have stated before the majority of humans are afraid of death. Even Jesus Christ himself feared death. Knowing this I do not see how anyone could cast the first stone. Now it is the year nineteen hundred and seventy-four and we have a new president, President Gerald Ford. President Ford has granted amnesty to all. That means that all offenders will be forgiven and are permitted to work their way back into society. But these people are not the only ones affected by this. Our former president, President Richard M. Nixon, has also been granted amnesty. This has really caused controversy among Americans. Most of them feel that two separate crimes against America have been committed. Some feel that since both committed crimes against America, they both should either be punished or both acquitted. But one thing we all can agree upon is that something should be done about this increase in crime in America. We cannot let this come about. But the former president of the United States is not the only one who has been controlled by greed. The president of the Teamster's Union, members of SCLC, a black organization, some black civil rights leaders, cashiers and other people have been effected by this dread disease that effects the black hearts of men. So you see this is nothing we can read about and forget. It has happened in the past. It is happening now in the present. And it will continue to happen in the future if we don't take action now. We can start by going to the polls and voting seriously. We must put men in office who want what we want, justice for all Americans. We can also get involved in the affairs of America. This is no time to be in the world and not of the world because it does effect everyone. Until we decide to take this issue seriously, corruption will forever rule the lifes of men. Until we decide to take any action against this evil, we shall suffer unnessarily. But when we do and all goodness comes through, these chains of evil which bind us now will be broken and honesty will no longer be a stranger to us, but look to us like a welcomed friend.

[Essay untitled]

The ivory dogwood petals float fragrantly in the breeze on the island between asphalt drives. The grass pushes back the black earth in its fight to get sunlight. All is still except for the occasionally passing of some flashing new cars. Paved streets are endings for endlessly regular tributaries. The sources of these tributaries are exquisite mansions and three car garages. The families wake at the call of a hired maid and receive breakfast at convenience. Dad hops into his car to go to his business; Mom slides into her new brilliant Pontiac, and the maid drives the kids to their exclusive school. With the mother gone to her card parties and hairdresser the house is empty except for the maid puttering about cleaning the twelve rooms. What a perfect family morning and such an idyllic mode of existence. There is none of the noisy traffic and crowded yards. "God's in his heaven all's right with the world."

The moss ekes out a mean living between the cracks in ancient sidewalks. Grass on lawns is a fantasy. The lawns are a few feet square, and are the only playground for the bare feet pading about them. Parking on the alley sized "streets" makes it hard to stay dry in spring rain. Murky pools in road ruts breed ever present mosquitoes. But there are no protective screens on broken pane windows. The families wake when they do. There are three families living in this three room mess. After women scrounge an inadequate repast, the husbands head out to find work; the mothers take the bus to the mansions where they are servants; the children walk to the dreary public school whose facade resembles the condemned brick buildings down the block. Day after day, the pulsating pattern varies but slightly. God's in his heaven, all's wrong with the world.

4. The Subjective Reaction Scale

Group size: Entire class in a large-group discussion circle.
Time required: Forty minutes for completing the questionnaire and
at least sixty minutes on another day for discussing student attitudes.
To save time, the questionnaires may be completed at home.
Materials: One copy of the subjective reaction scale (included at the
end of this strategy) to each student. This questionnaire asks the
student to rate the prestige value of sentences containing pompous
diction, slang words, usage choices, writing and spelling errors, and
black English features. The instrument is an adaptation of one used
by William Labov in *Social Stratification of English in New York City*
(Washington, D.C.: Center for Applied Linguistics, 1966).

Goals

A. To tabulate class attitudes toward various language features.
B. To encourage students to articulate their attitudes and ideas
    concerning "correctness" in language use.
C. To serve as a "stepping stone" to teaching students linguistic
    facts.

Process

A. Instructor does not explain goals of exercise until *after* the
    questionnaire is completed, since this is a "masked" or "guised"
    instrument. Students will think they are recording the worth or
    correctness of sentences, when actually they are recording their
    attitudes toward features in the sentences.
B. Students complete questionnaire.
C. A volunteer tabulates all responses at home and arrives at an
    "average" rating for each sentence. For example, the tabulator
    may find that the average rating for one item is at the factory
    worker level while another may be much higher.
D. On the next class day, the questionnaires are returned to the
    students, and the instructor leads a class discussion on why the
    writers of these sentences were rated low or high. Note: the
    students, not the instructor, should explain the high or low
    ratings.
E. Since student discussion can be easily stifled, the instructor
    should refrain from "correcting" false language notions at this

point; instead, he or she can make mental notes of points to cover at a later time.

Variations

A. Different sentences with varying features can be added to the questionnaire instrument.
B. Students may be asked to free write after this discussion.
C. Students may be asked to write a character description of the writer of a sentence of their choice. These character descriptions could be shared by students in small groups. This should be done before the large-group discussion.
D. After the large-group discussion, the teacher may want to discuss the statement *Students' Right to Their Own Language* (Urbana, Ill.: National Council of Teachers of English, 1974) and get student reaction.
E. The instructor may use the exercise as a springboard to lectures on the English language, geographical and social dialects, language attitudes, and "rules" of language usage.

Subjective Reaction Scale

Directions: Assume that you are the personnel director in charge of hiring all employees for a large factory and that the following sentences were each written by different people applying for jobs. Assign to each statement the letter of the job you think the applicant qualifies for. You wouldn't, of course, hire someone just on the basis of writing ability, but we are here measuring writing qualifications only. Your decision means that the writer could be hired for that job and all jobs below it, but could not—because of his or her writing—hold any jobs above that level.

A. Communications director
B. Office worker
C. Salesperson
D. Factory supervisor
E. Factory worker
F. None of these

_____ 1. It's been much too long since we last talked, and I'm really looking forward to your visit.

_____ 2. He always be messing around, so I just stop the weakly allowance.

_____ 3. Mr. Robbins who lived next door to us did not pain his house for fifteen years.

_____ 4. Baxter didn't like nothing about Army life.

_____ 5. I told the s.o.b. I'd kick his butt if he didn't leave Sally alone.

_____ 6. George say he in trouble over that report.

_____ 7. Jerry Rutherford was a broad-faced, heavy-set Irish boy who was the bully of the block, his favorite pastime seemed to be terrorizing boys only half his size.

_____ 8. Moses may have led the jews out of egypt, but it was Golda Meir who let the arabs know that isreal would never be conquered again.

_____ 9. I walk to school every day that first year at Barnsely.

_____10. I have never known anyone who could play chess with Mr. Dodds without losing patience.

_____11. He was studing hard to learn the issues because he wanted to be elected the class canidate.

_____12. He was trying to give me a snow job, but I wasn't about to be sucked in.

_____13. She left the party before anybody. Because she had to be home before midnight.

_____14. According to Belsham, one outstanding trait of the selfless person is the willingness to fight for a just cause a cause in which he or she stands to gain little and lose much.

_____15. A list of students whose health records indicate that such noted information should be brought to the attention of the college instructors will be kept in the office of Mr. Jones and Mr. Smith.

_____16. I gave him $30 & he only gave me back $5.

_____17. He said he didn't see nobody around the store last night.

_____18. I am desirous of meeting her, and when I do, I shall tell her how much we enjoy her music.

_____19. I got so mad that I told her to bug off!

_____20. It should not, I think, be too much of a strain on your resources (although I know that we are all under the burden of a tight budget) to furnish the required materials so that the project deadline can be met, thus forestalling other contractual penalties.

_____21. Although Bill was the youngest member there. He didn't even offer to go to the store for her.

_____22. The latter half of the nineteenth century saw an enormous effort directed toward adjusting, after Darwin's *The Origin of the Species*, to changed notions of humanity's relation to the rest of God's living creatures and hence to changed notions of the nature of humanity.

_____23. The teacher had the tesses turned wrong-side-up on
           our desses when we came in the room.
_____24. I should think it presumptuous of you to allow your
           predilection for bizarre clothing to alter the formality
           of this occasion.
_____25. Mr. Juard was the nicest person I've ever met he
           would always have a big smile and warm hello for
           everyone in the building.

5.   Sentence Deletion: Discovering Tacit Language Knowledge

Group size: This exercise can be used in either a large or small group, but small groups of four to five students are preferable.
Time required: Approximately one hour.
Materials: Copies of paragraphs, each of which has a sentence deleted, for each student in the group. (A sample is included at the end of this strategy.)

Goals

A. To show students how much they tacitly know about language use.
B. To encourage student thinking about written forms.
C. To build sentence confidence in using and discussing language.

Process

A. The instructor explains the goals of the exercise and distributes the paragraphs to students.
B. The instructor asks the students to read each paragraph, to create a sentence which would fit well in the blank space where the original sentence has been deleted, and to list clues in the paragraph which seem to demand the sentence each creates.
C. After the students have created sentences for the blank spaces, they discuss what clues they used from the paragraph to arrive at their sentence and come to a consensus on which of their sentences best fits the paragraph in terms of either content, diction, tone, and sentence style or the students' own concept of good paragraph development.
D. The instructor can point out, once student discussion has ended, how much they really *do* know about language use, because the exercises they have performed demand analytical reading for content, knowledge of tone, register, and syntax, and genuine creative ability.

Variations

A. Depending on the class level, the instructor may wish to begin with cloze exercises (leaving out only substantive words in a passage and having the students choose from four alternatives the word that best fits the sentence) or word deletion exercises (leaving out substantive words and having students come up with an appropriate word on their own) before using the sentence deletion exercise. An example of a word deletion exercise follows the example of a sentence deletion exercise. Caution: the instructor should discourage the idea that the "original" word or sentence is the "correct" one. Emphasis should be placed on *all* answers that fit well.

B.   Individual students or groups of students could create their own deletion or cloze exercises to try on classmates. Much language learning takes place during the creation of such exercises.

Sentence Deletion Exercise

The paragraphs below are adaptations from a student essay, "The Sheep and the Foxes," written by Joan Slaughter, a student at the Community College of Baltimore, Harbor Campus, Baltimore, Maryland. Any coherent, well-formed paragraph can be adapted for use in this exercise, but some care should be taken in choosing the sentence to delete; there should be many contextual clues pointing to the omitted information the deleted sentence contains.

1.   When it comes to negative female attitudes toward the feminist movement, there are two types of women: the foxes and the sheep. Some women are against the feminist movement because they have made the system work so well for them that they stand to lose by liberation. They are the foxes. [Deleted sentence] They are the sheep. (Deleted sentence is "Other women have followed societal values and mores without thinking.")

2.   The most adamant anti-feminists are the foxes. Patsy Perkins, for example, was a cheerleader in high school and homecoming queen in college. Pretty, vivacious, and well-built, she snared a highly successful physician and businessman. [Deleted sentence] Her role is to be a lovely, well-groomed and gracious hostess. That's nice work if you can get it. (Deleted sentence is "Wearing expensive clothes and driving a new Cadillac, she is her husband's human status symbol.")

Word Deletion Exercise

Substantive words have been removed from the following essay as an example of the sort of text that might be used for the exercise described in the variations section. A key to the deleted words follows the essay. The essay, written by Norman Mark, appeared in the Panorama section of the Chicago *Daily News*.

Women in TV-Land: You've Got
a Long Way to Go, Baby

You might think you've come a long way, __1__, but you __2__. At least not in TV commercials, prime-time programs and kiddie cartoons, according to studies published __3__ the spring issue of the *Journal of Communications* of the University of Pennsylvania.

Television fixes subtle pictures in our __4__, and its image of __5__, more often than not, is that of a drudge who adores the kitchen or bathroom.

In a study of TV __6__, two Canadian professors of marketing noted that the voice-overs, those authoritative people who tell you what to __7__, are men by 10-1.

We tend to see women selling deodorants, toothpaste or soap, but not gasoline or oil. When women do the __8__, they often demonstrate the product, such as by washing the floor.

When men sell to us, they often explain the product. Thus, the authors conclude, women in commercials "continue to __9__ house, launder, cook and serve meals, while the men __10__ the orders and advice and eat the meals." Females often get the comic roles, men the __11__ ones. The researchers __12__ that males in prime time __13__ generally more mature, more serious and __14__ likely to be employed than __15__. Males have adventures and get into violent situations. __16__ are usually powerful and smart. __17__ are presented as lacking independence. __18__ are not found in adventure situations; they are younger, more likely to be married and less __19__ to be employed.

Helen White Streecher, a senior research associate with the Illinois Department __20__ Mental __21__ in Chicago, looked __22__ kiddie cartoons and arrived at similar __23__. __24__ found that, in general, cartoon females were less numerous than __25__, made fewer appearances, had __26__ lines, played fewer bad roles, were __27__ active, occupied far fewer positions of responsibility, __28__ less money, and were more preponderantly juvenile than males.

"Mothers worked only in the __29__; males did not participate in housework. In many activities in which a girl showed some form of skill (e.g., cheerleading), her performance was duplicated by a __30__ or other pet."

Key to Deleted Words

1. baby	11. serious	21. Health
2. haven't	12. concluded	22. at
3. in	13. are	23. results
4. minds	14. more	24. She
5. women	15. women	25. males
6. recently	16. They	26. fewer
7. do	17. Women	27. less
8. selling	18. They	28. made
9. clean	19. likely	29. home
10. give	20. of	30. dog

6. Language Curiosities

Group size: Either a large or small group.
Time required: An entire week of class time can be spent on this activity; thirty to fifty minutes should be used to give instructions, build interest, and show examples of "language curiosities," and at least two ensuing class periods can be used for group discussion of "language curiosities" that class members have found.
Materials: Samples of "language curiosities" which the instructor can use as examples. (Some samples of actual student "discoveries" follow this strategy.)

Goals

A. To encourage students to become more aware of language use in their own immediate environment.
B. To encourage student discussion of language use for various purposes and audiences.

Process

A. The instructor briefly explains the goals of the activity and sets assignment limits—number of "language curiosities" to find and due dates—for the class.
B. The instructor reads some sample "language curiosities," discusses them in some depth, and points out possible areas where students might find "language curiosities" (bathroom walls, road and traffic signs, advertisements, letters to the editor, local colloquialisms, pronunciation differences of various words, etc.).
C. As a homework assignment, students collect their own examples of interesting, odd, or curious uses of language. It is important that this activity *not* become a competition to find the "best" example of curious language use for the instructor to judge; rather, it should stimulate students to think more about the language they hear and read every day and to discover for themselves what is "curious" and what is "normal" language use. Differences of opinion will become evident in class discussions.
D. On the following class day, the class members read their examples of language curiosities, and the entire class or small groups discuss these examples. The instructor should be aware that some of the student examples will spark little or no discussion, while other examples may lead into lengthy, far-reaching discussions about language which may require of the instructor a fair

knowledge of grammar, language history, and dialect differences. Other examples will stimulate spontaneous contributions from class or group members which are similar, in the students' minds, to the example under discussion.

E. The instructor may choose to give a second home assignment to collect more examples of curious language use. Since many students get very interested in this activity after the first class discussion, the second assignment gives them an opportunity to continue their reflections on language use in their own environment.

F. On the following class day, the class or group again discusses the new examples of language curiosities.

Variations

A. To save class time, these language discoveries can be recorded in a "language journal" to be turned in to the instructor, rather than be discussed in class.

B. Some students may choose to use tape recorders to record speech variations in their community.

C. Some students may prefer to prepare a dictionary of neologisms or slang words either currently in use or out of date. Some questions they may attempt to answer are: (1) What group invented the word or phrase? Why? (2) What does it mean? (3) What group(s) adopted the term? (4) What has happened to the word since it was invented? As a starting point for this variation, the instructor may wish to show students *A Dictionary of Slang and Unconventional English* (New York: Macmillan Co., 1970), edited by Eric Partridge, or *A Dictionary of Americanisms on Historical Principles* (Chicago: University of Chicago Press, 1956), edited by Mitford Mathews.

Sample Language Curiosities

The following examples were written by students at various levels in classes where we have used the Language Curiosity strategy.

1. Why do we use the same sound or pronunciation to mean two totally different things, but spell them differently in writing? For example, "bare" and "bear" are pronounced the same but spelled differently. That may be obvious enough, but why do we have two or more different meanings for "bear?" In one sense, we use it to mean a big furry animal and in another sense, we use it to mean "turn"—as in "bear to the right"—or "stick with"—as in "bear with me."

Not knowing the spelling difference between these two words *could* get one in trouble. For example, what if someone wrote "Bare with me"?

2. Why do people from Massachusetts never use the letter 'r' when they talk? They pronounce "car" as if it were spelled "cah," "park" as if it were spelled "pahk," and "aunt" as if it were spelled "auhnt"? Are they trying to impress everyone? By the way, why does Archie Bunker pronounce "toilet" as if it were spelled "terlet?"

3. A sign on Reston Street reads, "Slow children crossing". I wonder if they are physically slow or mentally slow? Either way, drivers may want to hold down their speed on this street!

4. Another sign reads, "No truck parking beyond this point enforced." Truck drivers must feel very secure when they pull their rigs into *that* parking lot!

5. A religious sign, seen along many roads in the South, reads: "Jesus saves." I know the message that is meant, but I also can't help thinking that banks will go to *any* lengths in their advertisements!

6. Why does the word "no" begin with the letter "n" in so many languages? In English it is "no," in French it is "non," in German it is "nein," and in Russian it is "nyet."

7. On the bus to school everyday, I go crazy trying to decide if the company who made the bus spells its name "Flxible" or "Fixible." If it is the first spelling, how do you pronounce it?

8. I remember my senior English teacher saying that "like" was a preposition. Yet it can also be a verb when used "I like her a lot." Am I right?

9. A traffic sign on Madison Avenue reads "Left Lane must turn left." I wonder if the left lane *knows* that?

Prewriting

Before we ever put pen to paper to write, we go through a process which, for lack of a better term, is called prewriting. Admittedly, this process is not defined neatly, but there seem to be three elements or steps in the prewriting process. First, most of our writing comes as a response to someone or something, that is, our experience compels us to communicate. The second step emanates from this need to respond: we focus on a topic to discuss and very often identify clearly who our audience is. Prewriting ends when we determine what form our writing is to take and what manner or organization is best suited to our topic and audience. Obviously, in the normal process of prewriting, these steps do not occur in this precise, linear order. In fact, the prewriting stage is such an amorphous, unexplored domain that it is impossible to chart one course that could guide all would-be writers.

The waters of this prewriting domain remain murky because the domain is inside the individual writer's head. Despite the advances of post-Freudian psychiatry and psychology, too little is known of the individual psyche—and its similarity to other psyches—for all-inclusive principles to be stated. While some poets and novelists have written accounts of their own prewriting or discovery experiences over the years, little attempt was made before the mid-twentieth century to discover if systematic procedures (other than the obligatory outline) could be taught that would help neophyte writers to invent or discover their own voices, their own ideas, and their own experiences in order to communicate them.

Fortunately, a renewed interest in rhetoric has emerged in the last two decades, spurred on partly by advances in psychology and transformational-generative linguistics and partly by the notion that the "old" rhetoric simply wasn't adequate. This renewed interest has led to new approaches to teaching writing, some of which (for example, Rohman and Wlecke's *Pre-Writing: The Construction and Application of Models for Concept Formation in Writing* [East Lansing, Mich.: Michigan State University, U.S. Office of Education Cooperative Research Project No. 2174, 1964] and Young, Becker, and Pike's *Rhetoric: Discovery and Change* [New York: Harcourt Brace and World, 1970]) offer a complete philosophy of composition, put a major emphasis on the prewriting stage, and offer solid heuristic strategies for teaching the prewriting process.

Like the philosophy of both works mentioned above, our philosophy of prewriting centers on engaging students in the writing process and helping them discover what is important or true for them on any given subject at any given time (we will steer away from such fancy labels as "integration of experience" or "self-actualization").

Unfortunately, no one has found the perfect system for teaching the prewriting process, but that fact does not deter teachers from trying new classroom strategies on prewriting. If teachers expect students to become capable writers, they must help them develop prewriting skills. Some students, of course, will have stumbled onto their own methods; but for the truly inexperienced writers, teachers must not only motivate them to write (and write better), but also show them ways of discovering concepts, experiences, and ideas and gathering materials for their writing.

What moves us to write obviously must come from our own experience. From Chaucer to Faulkner, all writers have been moved to write by experiences, people, or insights that have somehow touched them. In the same way, students have had moving experiences, met fascinating people, and have had flashes of insight. Therefore, they do have subject matter or topics for their writings. If teachers have made them feel comfortable in class, then using their own experiences for writing will come more naturally to them.

Students may be self-motivated writers, or they may be moved to write by the assignment of an essay. In most instances, teachers are the motivating force. Perhaps the best teachers can expect is that by the end of their courses, students will feel more self-motivation. To arrive at this point, students must develop the next step in the compositional process: identifying topics and audiences.

When we speak of identifying a topic, we are describing a much bigger task than most students imagine. A student may wish to write an attack on the school administration, but if he or she has no supporting material, the writer has not sufficiently identified a writable topic. Therefore, the student must collect data, examples, reasons, and facts in order to really comprehend the topic. Many of the exercises in this section are designed to increase awareness of intra- and extrapersonal issues and to develop student skills for using experience as writing material. Ideally, these strategies will both motivate students to write and generate the material about which to write.

You will notice that we do not suggest lists of topics. Our thinking is that one of the fundamental skills for writers is generating their own topics. If students come to expect that a teacher will provide a topic, then they have been made dependent. In the type of strategy given in this chapter, many topics will be generated. Because the exercises in many cases involve small groups, students often become motivated to write responses produced by animated discussions.

Once we have settled on a topic and have gathered material to write about, our next task is to discover our audience. Again, this is an oft neglected area of study. Experienced writers would not use the same register (i.e., level of formality), especially vocabulary, in a letter to their mother that they would use in writing to a business. They subconsciously choose the correct register for their audience. While in most instances, the students' audience will be a teacher or their classmates, they should become keenly aware of and know how to write to different audiences. For most students, writing to an audience will come with a realization that they must consider an audience in writing. We have included two strategies that facilitate writing to particular audiences.

The final step of the prewriting process is that of making formal choices. Prior to actually writing, writers must decide what form their material is to take. The topic and the audience will help determine choice of form. Yet, it is important for the student to know that any topic can be written about in many ways—narration, analysis, comparison, description, persuasion, or opinion—depending on the writer's *purpose* for writing. Does the writer wish to persuade, to entertain, to describe? Having made this choice, the writer must then choose appropriate materials; if, for example, the writer wishes to write an opinion essay, he or she must choose examples, reasons, and facts. Once the topic, audience, and form are chosen, only one part of the prewriting process is left: selecting a method of organization. An opinion essay may be organized in many ways—forming a thesis statement and listing particular reasons or starting from a particular example and developing a general conclusion are just two ways to form an opinion essay. The same choices for development are found in other types of writings.

Several of the strategies in this section integrate all of the activities of the first stage of the writing process. We have used these strategies with our students and have found them effective in teaching students to generate topics, identify audiences, and make the formal choices necessary for good writing.

1. Value Exploration

Group size: Small groups of about six students.

Time required: Usually about fifty minutes. You may wish to reduce the number of questions or add more; if you do either, the time will vary.

Materials: Duplicated copies of the value choices questions with instructions (a sample is included at the end of this strategy). If you wish the students to jot down summary examples or reasons discussed by other members of the groups, each student will need a pen and some paper.

Goals

A. To facilitate the making of difficult decisions about the course of one's life.
B. To generate ideas, experiences, and examples for essay writing.
C. To motivate students to write from their experience by involving the total person, cognitive and affective.
D. To encourage mutual exchange among class members, thereby increasing students' comfort in the classroom setting.
E. To introduce or review the process of finding a topic by asking questions, making decisions, and reflecting on past experiences.

Process

A. Discuss the goals of the strategy with the class.
B. Split them into groups, or allow them to split up.
C. Pass out the instructions and the questions.
D. Read the instructions and ask for questions.
E. Give them some time to complete the questions.
F. When the questions are completed, the small groups may begin sharing their responses.
G. (Optional) The teacher may wish to sit in with each group and share his or her answers. Try to sit in on all the groups, even if briefly, because in doing so, you will raise their comfort level with you and you will gain some insight about your students.
H. When all of the groups seem to have finished their discussions, or when time is almost gone for the small-group segment of the strategy, you may wish to have a general class discussion. While any appropriate question may be discussed, here are some that you might use:
    1. Which questions were the hardest for you to answer?

2. Which questions had the most immediate importance for you?
3. Which question caused the greatest variety of opinion in your group? Why?
4. Which question caused you to think of the subject for the first time?

I. Once the class discussion is over, you might wish to remind the students that any of these questions are good topic sentences; that the ideas and experiences they have shared in the groups can be used as supporting reasons or examples in their writing; and that this process of raising a question and gathering ideas from experience is directly applicable to writing.

Variations

A. You may have students fill out the form at home if you wish to save time in class.
B. You might tell them to outline some reasons for their position on each question. If you do this, we suggest that you give only a few questions.
C. You might write one of the questions on the board and then outline, from the class response, all of the reasons and examples brought up in answering that question. Then on the board organize the examples into an essay outline, showing them how to develop an essay from their ideas.
D. The process described in variation C can be done in the small groups.
E. Each small group can be instructed to arrive at a consensus answer to one of the questions; then they can write an outline of all of their reasons for the consensus decision. This outline can be reported to the class and/or written on the board. Students can then use this outline for their next essay.
F. Make up questions for the choices sheet that are more immediately pertinent to your class. An excellent source for value choice questions is Sidney Simon, Leland Howe, and Howard Kirschenbaum, *Values Clarification: A Handbook of Practical Strategies for Teachers and Students* (New York: Hart Publishing Co., 1972). The sample values questionnaire that follows is an adaptation of material found in *Values Clarification*, pp. 58ff.

Values Questionnaire

We make choices constantly. Listed below are some questions; put a check next to the answer that most nearly represents how you feel and think about the question. Then, share your responses with the group: perhaps you will wish to tell why you made the choice that you did—give reasons or examples from your experience. OF COURSE YOU MAY *PASS* ON A QUESTION, IF YOU WISH. Remember, everyone in a group has a right to his or her own opinion, so listen carefully to the others. In doing so, you might learn more about yourself.

1. Of the following characteristics, which do you think is most important for a friend of yours?
   a. Honesty
   b. A willingness to share
   c. Loyalty
2. Which would you least like to have?
   a. Little money
   b. Poor health
   c. A crippled body
3. If you were a member of the Senate, to which of the following would you give most concern?
   a. Defense
   b. The nation's poor
   c. Exploring for fuel
4. If your father died and you had your own family, what would you do for your aging mother?
   a. Have her come live with you
   b. Admit her into a nursing home
   c. Get her an apartment of her own
5. Which of these is the worst problem in the local area today?
   a. Malnutrition
   b. Overcrowding
   c. Unemployment
   d. Discrimination by race or sex
6. Which of these would be hardest for you?
   a. Your father's death
   b. Your death
   c. A close friend's death
7. Which of the following do you value more?
   a. Wisdom
   b. Love
   c. World peace
8. Which would you rather do on your vacation?
   a. Go to the relatives for a visit
   b. Head to Colorado with some friends
   c. Stay at home and relax

2. Consensus Decision Making

Group size: Small groups of around six members.
Time required: Depends on the number of issues upon which students are to deliberate. If they are given one of the issues suggested here, the small groups will need about fifty minutes for decision making.
Materials: A duplicated copy for each student of the issue(s) to be decided with the instructions for this strategy (sample decision-making tasks are included at the end of this strategy).

Goals

A. To facilitate the making of decisions about common writing issues.
B. To aid students in gathering topics and ideas for essays.
C. To put them in touch with their past experiences for their writing.
D. To increase their awareness of themselves.
E. To promote constructive interaction among class members, thereby increasing the rapport among the students.

Process

A. Explain the goals and instructions of this strategy.
B. Distribute the duplicated instructions.
C. Give students a short time to read the instructions and to fill out the rank ordering.
D. Discuss any questions about the exercise.
E. Split into small groups and let them begin the decision making.
F. Remind them of the time limit for the decision making, which will depend on the issue to be decided.
G. Observe groups and sit in with them if you wish. However, we suggest that you do not enter into the decision making.
H. After time is up or when they are finished, let each group report their decision to the entire class.
I. You may wish to allow for class discussion of the issue.
J. Emphasize that all of the reasons and examples used in discussion may be used in essays. Remind students that their own experience is a rich mine of essay material, as was evidenced by the group discussions. You might wish to review ways of outlining an essay from the material discussed.

Variations

A. You might have the students outline reasons for their positions before coming to class and then have them add to their lists during the discussion.
B. The small groups might each write a position paper combining all member contributions and describing the rationale for their conclusions.
C. A reporter might be selected from each group to form another small group, composed of the reporters from all the groups and the instructor, which then discusses the topic at hand.
D. If the discussion topics listed in the next section do not seem pertinent to your class, you can use almost any relevant issue for the exercise. For instance, we once participated in a consensus decision-making process in a graduate course where the issue was whether or not we should have coffee made for our class—a very stimulating and provocative issue to us. An excellent source of consensus decision-making exercises is J. William Pfeiffer and John E. Jones, *A Handbook of Structured Experiences for Human Relations Training*, 6 vols. (Iowa City: University Associates Press, 1973–77).
E. You may just let the students decide if true consensus is possible.

Tasks

The issues suggested here for decision making are ones commonly used in the context of small-group training. However, as you can see, they provide good stimulation for student discussion. Before students begin the decision making, these instructions might help:

1. State your position as logically as you can. Stay open to other people's logic. Try to think of *reasons* for your decisions.

2. Don't change your mind just to come to agreement and to avoid conflict. You ought to be able to agree at least a little with the final outcome.

3. Avoid "conflict reducing" techniques such as majority voting, averaging, or trading, that is, giving in on one decision as long as others give in on the next decision.

4. Look upon differences of opinion as helpful in decision making.

Task A. Rank each of the values listed below in the order in which most of the people your age would list them. For example, you might say that wisdom is valued highest, followed by happiness and so on until all the values are ranked. Once all group members have made their orderings, the group should arrive at a consensus ranking of the values.

_____ Pleasure

_____ Wisdom

_____ Mature love

_____ Self-respect

_____ World peace

_____ Freedom

_____ Family stability

_____ Happiness

Task B. Rank the following aims of education from the most important to the least important. Make your decision from your own point of view. Once all group members are finished, the group should arrive at a consensus listing.

_____ To become a good citizen

_____ To gain a job skill

_____ To become a better person

_____ To learn correct behavior

_____ To understand our culture and heritage

_____ To learn how to make decisions

_____ (Add one of your own here)

Task C. Bring to class a list of the five biggest problems facing people your age. In your groups rank the problems listed by each member from the biggest problem to the smallest problem using consensus decision making.

Task D. Rank the following crisis situations from the most traumatic to you to the least. You should think of reasons and examples for your ranking to help your group understand your position. After each group member has completed the questionnaire, the rankings should be shared with the group. Then, the group should decide by consensus a group ordering of the crises.

_____ Divorce

_____ Unwanted pregnancy

_____ Being fired from a job

_____ Death of your wife or husband

_____ Death of a close friend

_____ Moving of your family

_____ Sickness or injury to yourself

(The teacher may add other crises to this list or make up an entirely different list.)

Task Variations

A. Give your students any problem that demands a choice; put
   them in groups and let them come to a consensus decision.
   Instruct them to have a reporter outline the reasons for the final
   decision. When all groups are finished, outline on the board all
   of the reasons and examples given; put this into the form of an
   opinion or analysis essay. Try to select a topic about which they
   will have strong feelings and much information, e.g., something
   around school, in the city, or in the classroom.
B. You might have students record ideas and experiences that were
   discussed as an "idea bank" for their future use. You might
   instruct them to develop an essay from the discussion.

3. The Fish Bowl: Writing about What You See

Group size: The inner group will usually consist of volunteers representing each small group and, if you wish, yourself.
Time required: Explanation of roles takes thirty minutes; the exercise itself runs concurrently with the consensus decision-making exercises described in strategies one and two.
Materials: Whatever sheet used to make the consensus decision in the small groups.

Goals

A. To generate ideas and examples for opinion and/or analysis essays.
B. To provide an opportunity for the class to observe a group making a consensus decision.
C. To learn more about roles necessary for making a group work well.
D. To provide a forum for the discussion of important questions.

Process

A. This exercise is an outgrowth of any of the consensus decision-making exercises given in this book or of your own design.
B. After the consensus decision-making exercise is completed by the small groups, ask each group to select one member to represent them in an inner group that will arrive at a consensus decision about the issue at hand.
C. Representatives and the instructor should form a circle to discuss the decision; other class members should form a circle around this inner group.
D. Now give out the group observation form. (A sample is shown on p. 37.)
E. Give one of the following sets of instructions or ones of your own formulation, depending on the type of writing assignment you wish to have come from this exercise.
    1. "The sheet given out lists seven important roles that help a group function effectively. [At this point, you may wish to read through the group observation form and then ask for questions to check the students' understanding of these roles.] While those of us in the inner circle try to come to a consensus decision, your function is to observe the group as it works together. In a moment, I will give you the name of one member to observe. Each time this person participates in the discussion, note on the sheet which role the person is

taking by writing down the first few words in the blank next to the appropriate category. For example, if someone begins a comment by saying 'Our group took this position because . . . . ,' you would record just these words in the blank next to the 'contributing' heading. By observing the persons in the inner circle in this way, you will be able to analyze helpful group behaviors. When the group discussion is over, you will be asked to write an analysis of the roles taken by the person you observed using specific examples taken from your observer sheet."

2.   Or, give these instructions: "Observe the group carefully, listening for reasons and examples given for each position taken. Take your own notes. When the group has finished, you should write an essay stating your opinion on this issue. Use the reasons and examples given in the discussion as well as those of your own."

F.   (Optional) When the inner group is finished, you might have the observers in the outer circle give them feedback as to how they took the roles listed on the group observation form. This feedback might be given orally or in a written report.

Variations

A.   An "open chair" may be used in the exercise. That is, leave one empty chair in the inner circle; class members may fill the chair to raise points that have not been considered. One caution: the "open chair" participants can sometimes distract the inner group and slow their process down.

B.   You might instruct the members of the inner group to take only one or two assigned roles. For instance, one member might only contribute and encourage.

C.   If the observers are going to concentrate on the process of the group discussion (the first set of directions in step E of the process section), you might want to send the inner circle members out of the room while the instructions are given to the class. If the inner group members are aware that they are being observed individually, they could be distracted. However, let them know that they are being observed.

D.   You might want to remind the observers that some comments will fall outside of the categories on the observer sheet and therefore cannot be recorded.

E.   The observer sheets might be discussed before doing any of the consensus decision-making exercises. Knowledge of helping roles might aid students in their group work.

Group Observation Form

Group Building Roles	Person Observed
1. *Initiating*: getting the process started; beginning discussion.	
2. *Contributing*: sharing of opinions, pertinent information, and ideas; giving examples.	
3. *Gatekeeping*: trying to make it possible for another member to make a contribution to the group or suggesting limited talking time for everyone so that all will have a chance to be heard.	
4. *Standard Setting*: suggesting procedures to follow; reminding group of time limits; keeping discussion on the topic.	
5. *Summarizing*: summarizing what the group feeling is sensed to be; describing reactions of the group to ideas or solutions.	
6. *Encouraging*: being friendly, warm, responsive to others; praising others and their ideas.	
7. *Following*: going along with decisions of the group; thoughtfully accepting the ideas of others; serving as audience during group discussion by closely listening.	

4. A Personal Road Map

Group size: Small groups of four or five members.
Time required: Approximately forty-five minutes.
Materials: One large sheet of newsprint for each student.

Goals

A. To help students discover significant personal experiences for narrative writing.
B. To encourage group and class cohesiveness and group sharing of experiences.

Process

A. After small groups are formed, the instructor asks the students to place a *B* (for birth) in a bottom corner of the sheet and a *P* (for the present) in a top corner of the sheet.
B. The instructor tells the students to think back across their lives to their birth and to draw a "road" (i.e., a line) from the *B* to the *P* that represents the course of their lives. It may be a straight line, a wavy line, a line that runs in circles, a line that has many detours, a line that has many dead ends, and so on.
C. The instructor asks students to place little drawings or pictures along that road to symbolize or indicate any experience—either good or bad, important or unimportant—that they remember from their lives.
D. When the "maps" are completed, students who are willing should be encouraged to explain these maps to their small groups, but *only* those who are willing to share should be asked to do so.
E. After the discussions, the instructor should point out that these symbols on the sheet all represent excellent topics for narrative writing, that they need only be shaped into words.

Variations

A. The instructor could ask the students to put in more symbols at home as new memories of experiences are recalled. The map, then, can be a useful "storehouse" of topics for future narrative writings.
B. Narratives written by students in previous classes might be duplicated, with the student writer's permission, and distributed

to the class. The instructor might wish to talk with the class about chronological order in narrative writing, use of dialogue and description, and the like.

C. This exercise may be a good one to introduce the subject of autobiography, which is further pursued in the strategies Life Planning, Self-disclosure: Ideas for Narration, and Value Exploration.

5. Self-disclosure: Ideas for Narration

Group size: Small groups of about six students.
Time required: Usually about ninety minutes. If the posters are done outside of class, the exercise may not take as long.
Materials: The instructions for doing the posters; a large piece of paper, preferably newsprint; felt-tipped marker, pen, or crayon.

Goals

A. To help students delve into their experiences for narrative writing material.
B. To continue working on a foundation for openness in the group.
C. To open the students to dealing with group and class norms, for instance, to listen and not interrupt; to express feelings; to say what one means; to be honest; to include each member in discussions and value his or her contributions; to "own" one's feelings, i.e., knowing that one's feelings may not be shared by others and that their feelings are valid and authentic for them.

Process

A. Discuss the goals of the strategy with the class.
B. Split them into groups, or allow them to split up.
C. Pass out the instructions for the exercise.
D. Read the instructions to the class, answering questions as they arise: "With your marker, draw lines dividing the page into six spaces. In space number one, draw a symbol of the most significant event in the first half of your life; in space two, a symbol of the most important event in the second half of your life; in space three, the most significant event of the last year; in space four, that situation, activity, or whatever which you currently find most difficult or frustrating; in space five, that emotion which you find most difficult to express; and in space six, what you would do if you knew you had but three years to live and God, or whatever you believe controls all things, made it possible for you to do whatever you wanted to do. SHARE IN THESE SYMBOLS ONLY WHAT YOU WANT TO SHARE WITH YOUR GROUP because you will be asked to explain your poster."

Strategy five was inspired by Dr. Alberta Goodman, Miami–Dade Community College, Miami, Florida.

E. Be sure the students understand that they are to draw symbols; reassure them that they will be explaining the drawings, so they do not have to be artists.

F. When the students have finished drawing their posters, read the next instructions: "Now that you have finished drawing your posters, select one member of your group whom you want to know better. With this other person, find a separate place to share your posters. Taking turns, explain each symbol on your poster to your partner. Be sure to listen very closely to your partner because you will be asked afterward to explain his or her poster to the entire small group." After the instructions have been read, ask for questions from the students.

G. When all pairs seem to be finished sharing their posters, read the last part of the instructions: "Now move back into your small group. In turn, each person should carefully explain the poster of his or her partner to the rest of the small group. If the person explaining gets stuck, his or her partner may help out. Clarifying questions may be asked after the entire poster has been explained. The exercise is complete when the posters of all group members have been explained."

H. The instructor may wish to share his or her poster with the class at this time (or perhaps at the beginning of the exercise).

I. When all of the groups seem to have finished their discussions or when time is almost gone for the small groups, you may wish to have a general class discussion about the activity. Here are some questions that you might use:

    1. Which space was most difficult to fill? Why?
    2. What emotion did most people find difficult to express? Why?
    3. What situation do most people find difficult right now? Why?
    4. Were there any common desires about how people in your group wanted to spend the last three years of life?
    5. Were there any differences between the emotions men and women found most difficult to express? If so, why? (If there are obvious differences, the students may wish to spend time pursuing a discussion on this issue.)
    6. How did you feel about sharing this material?

J. At this point, you might wish to point out that any one section of the poster could be used as subject matter for a narrative. Especially pertinent to narrative writing would be poster spaces one, two, and three. However, students may wish to write a narrative example of an event that illustrates how difficult it is to express a certain emotion. Or, they might imagine one of the things they would wish to do if they had but three years to live and write a narrative describing that experience.

K. If you have not explained such matters as use of dialogue or chronological order, you might wish to do so.

Variations

A. If you do not wish to have students make posters, you might have them write an outline or even a paragraph about each item given in the directions for drawing the poster. Then they can read their paragraphs or explain their responses using the outlines. With this procedure, the splitting into pairs could be skipped. On the other hand, in order to practice listening skills, the partners might read and explain their six-part profile to each other. Then each person can share his or her partner's profile with the group.

B. If you wish to have your students write an essay of analysis, they can analyze the following topics suggested by this exercise:
    1. What I would do if I knew I was going to die.
    2. How events shape our lives.
    3. Why_____is the most difficult emotion for me to express (*men* or *women* might be substituted for *me*).
    4. Why_____is the most difficult situation for me to handle; or, Why_____is a difficult situation for people.

C. Students might just write reports using the material shared in class; for instance, they might report on the emotions their class found difficult to handle.

D. You might encourage students to jot down their own notes about material shared if they are going to write an analysis of some aspect of the exercise. However, you should remind them that material shared in class is to be kept in class; confidentiality is a fundamental norm for interpersonal communication.

E. Group members may wish to talk with each other about their feelings during this exercise, so some time might be given for this.

F. If your class is reading essays, you might use this exercise as an introduction to the autobiographical essay.

G. You might also wish to use this exercise to discuss the relationship between self-disclosure and the fears that often accompany writing. Some questions might be:

1. How is the process of this exercise like the process of writing an essay?
2. How could writing or sharing like this be seen as a threat by someone?
3. Questions of your own.

H. A good source for more ideas about self-disclosure and writing is the chapter "Self-disclosure, the Writer and the Reader" in Sidney M. Jourard, *The Transparent Self* (New York: Van Nostrand Reinhold, 1971).

6. Life Planning

Group size: Small groups of about six students.
Time required: Sixty to ninety minutes; allow more time if the worksheets are to be filled out during class time.
Materials: Duplicated copies of the life-planning questions with the instructions. (A sample is included at the end of this strategy.)

Goals

A. To assist students in exploring who they are and where they wish to go.
B. To help students gather information for writing an autobiographical essay or an analysis.
C. To facilitate self-disclosure among group members.

Process

A. Discuss the goals of the exercise with the students.
B. Have the students fill out the life-planning worksheet. Remind them that the information on this sheet will be shared with their group; therefore, they should only include information that they are willing to discuss with the other group members.
C. When all students have completed the worksheet, split the class up into groups of around six.
D. Give these instructions: "Now that you have completed the worksheet, share your responses with the members of your small group. All members should share their responses to item one before moving to item two. Take turns. Remember that the responses to the questionnaire are to be respected as the honest description of how the other members see certain aspects of themselves. Therefore, no judgement on our part is appropriate. Clarifying questions might be asked, but the student sharing his or her remarks has the right to answer in any way he or she wants."
E. (Optional) The teacher may wish to sit in with each group and share his or her answers. Try to sit in on all the groups, even if briefly, because in doing so, you will gain insights about your students.
F. When all of the groups seem to have finished their discussions,

Strategy six is an adaptation of an exercise in J. William Pfeiffer and John E. Jones, *A Handbook of Structured Experiences for Human Relations Training,* 6 vols. (Iowa City: University Associates Press, 1973–77), 2:101–12.

you may wish to have a general class discussion. Here are some questions that you might use:

1. Was there a reluctance to use complimentary adjectives in describing your career, personal affiliations, or personal development? If so, why?
2. What is the effect of concentrating on those personal qualities that you need to improve?
3. Did you have trouble filling out this questionnaire? Why?
4. Did you learn anything new about yourself while doing this exercise?
5. Did you learn anything new about the goals of the other people in class or in your group? Could you make any general conclusions about the goals of most people in the class?
6. Which aspect of the exercise did you find most provocative? Most difficult? Most helpful?
7. Do most people you know have clear goals in life?
8. Any questions that arise during class discussion.

G. After this discussion, you might wish to have your students use the content of the questionnaire to write essays. Here are some suggested topics.

1. Goals of my life.
2. A self-profile: who am I right now?
3. An essay giving examples of how the adjectives asked for on the questionnaire apply to one's career, personal affiliations, or personal development.
4. The qualities of a well-rounded person.
5. A character profile of someone possessing the qualities I wish most of all to possess.
6. A complete autobiography.
7. How one aspect of myself has changed over the last few years.
8. Any topic that fits into your class plan.

H. If you assign a topic, you may wish to spend some time describing ways of outlining an essay on the topic. Also, you might again remind students of the importance of raising universal questions that come from particular experiences: any authentic human experience is universal.

Variations

A. The worksheet could be filled out at home.
B. You might tell students to outline a particular example of how

one of the adjectives they use to describe themselves is fitting. This example might be shared with the group. Examples might be prepared for one adjective in each of the three categories.

C. The strategy might be used at the beginning of the semester and then repeated at the very end of the course. Comparisons and contrasts might be shown. Then students might be asked to write a comparison essay describing how they have changed over the course of the semester. A class discussion could be conducted on the forces at work that have helped people change.

D. The worksheet could be completed and used by individual students as source material for writing without being shared with class members.

E. More material may come out of this exercise than can be used in one essay. Therefore, several essays might be worked around this strategy.

Sample Questionnaire

If you wish to have students write or outline an example of how one of the adjectives fits them, you might include this instruction on the questionnaire and allow more space under each item.

Profile: My Life and Goals

1. List ten adjectives which describe yourself with respect to your career. Share the list with your group.

    _____   _____
    _____   _____
    _____   _____
    _____   _____
    _____   _____

2. List ten adjectives which describe yourself in regards to your personal relationships with family and friends. Share the list with your group.

    _____   _____
    _____   _____
    _____   _____
    _____   _____
    _____   _____

3. List ten adjectives which describe yourself in regards to your personal development. Share the list with your group.

    _____   _____
    _____   _____
    _____   _____
    _____   _____
    _____   _____

4. What are your career goals? List ten; use your imagination. What would be the ultimate successes in your career? Example: "I want to be the president of a large university." Share these goals with your group.

    _____
    _____
    _____
    _____
    _____
    _____
    _____
    _____
    _____
    _____

5. What goals do you have for yourself in regards to your relationships with family and friends—maybe even with people you regard as enemies? List ten and remember these are ideal successes, so be free in your selection of goals. Example: "I hope to establish complete mutual trust with my parents." Share these goals with your group.

    _____
    _____
    _____
    _____
    _____
    _____
    _____
    _____
    _____
    _____

6. What goals do you have for your personal development? Again, these should be ideals. List ten below in summary form. Example: "I want to be the best amateur golfer in the city." Share these goals with your group.

    _____
    _____
    _____
    _____
    _____
    _____
    _____
    _____
    _____
    _____

7. The Nature of the Mind

Group size: Entire class as a group (twenty-five to thirty).
Time required: Fifty minutes.
Materials: Copies of the two essays discussed below. Pen and paper are needed for the last half of the exercise.

Goals

A. To help students to see more about how the mind functions.
B. To encourage them to better understand how their experiences have shaped their ideas.
C. To allow them to use experiences as means of understanding themselves.
D. To open new means of interpreting how experiences have shaped them and also how they can use experience to make decisions in their lives.
E. To free up students' feelings about themselves by sharing pivotal events in their lives.

Process

A. This prewriting exercise is based on the contrast of two basic views of how the mind functions. An adequate summary of John Locke's view can be found in "The Mind as White Paper" from Book II of *An Essay Concerning Human Understanding*. Will Durant interprets Immanuel Kant's position clearly in "Kant and the Mind as Shaping Agent" from *The Story of Philosophy* (New York: Simon and Schuster, 1961). Both of these selections are brief enough to be copied for students to read (but see the note in the Introduction on reproducing copyrighted materials for classroom use). The essential contrast of the two views is between the mind as passive receiver or active agent.

   Locke views knowledge as the by-product of experience—both observation of sense experience and reflection on the operation of the mind. One source of ideas is sensation and the other is reflection. Thus, sense impression of external objects and the internal process of contemplation of these objects are the origin of all knowledge.

   For Kant, the mind is not merely a passive tablet written upon by experience and sensation, but it is an active agent that shapes

Strategy seven was contributed by Mary Dean, Shelby State Community College, Memphis, Tennessee.

sensations into ideas and transforms chaotic experiences into an ordered unity of thought. The mind transforms experience into knowledge or perception through its shaping power. Thus, the mind is an active agent which draws on sensations and experience to shape perceptions and ideas and to direct and use those ideas as it chooses.

B. Have students read the essays before class. Then begin a general discussion of the two essays.

C. Jot down on the board the students' comments about the two different views of how the mind functions, and categorize these views into two columns.

D. Move the discussion toward the students, personalizing the readings by having them relate experiences which in some way shaped or molded them. (Locke)

E. Then ask about experiences they have had that have allowed them to make decisions of a shaping nature in their lives. In other words, how has experience been an active force in encouraging independent, positive action and not just a force which acted upon them? (Kant)

F. After the discussion has subsided and all students have contributed who wish to, introduce the writing project described below. (The discussion should take about thirty minutes; the writing should take twenty minutes.)

G. Have students write two paragraphs—one that describes an experience in their lives that has shaped them in a certain way and another that describes an experience that has provoked a change in attitude or a course of action on their part.

H. After these two paragraphs are written, the students should better understand the complexity of how the mind functions and should be more comfortable about using experiences to both interpret themselves and find ways to actively make decisions in their lives.

Variations

A. Small groups can be used for the class discussion.

B. Instead of distributing the essays to students, you may wish to summarize the views yourself and interpret them for the class.

C. A way of introducing this exercise might be to set the two views in the context of the Age of Reason and the Romantic Age and discuss the contrasts of these two periods, particularly how the two views of the mind are reflective of these periods.

D. Instead of writing paragraphs, you may just have the students list as many life experiences as they can that conform to each of these views of the mind.

E. This exercise is good to use as a preliminary for an exercise on sense experience because many of the comments during discussion will probably relate to the sense experience of students. You may want to emphasize sense experiences in this exercise and focus on them in the next.

8. Sense Experience

Group size: Entire class (twenty-five to thirty).
Time required: Fifty minutes.
Materials: Blindfold; something to taste; something to smell.

Goals

A. To concretize sense experience for students.
B. To help them draw out vague impressions in a specific way.
C. To encourage willingness to talk about sight, taste, touch, smell, and sound.
D. To focus on the importance of firsthand sense experience by allowing it to be an end in itself.
E. To encourage the use of specific sense experience in writing through first having this experience as an end in itself.
F. To help students in interpersonal relations in a classroom setting by encouraging them to see, touch, and hear things as a group.

Process

A. Discuss the goals of the sense experience exercise with the class.
B. Begin with visual experience. Divide the class into two or more groups to analyze the scenes inside and outside the classroom.
C. Then ask each group to list features and qualities of what they see inside—e.g., furniture, clothes, people, accessories, paint, wood, metal, hair—and outside—e.g., the scene in the street.
D. Have the students study individuals carefully and report what they see; often they will see things they have never noticed before about their classmates.
E. Have all the students close their eyes and listen silently for one minute; then list on the board all the sounds they heard.
F. Have them close their eyes again and pass around something pungent to smell or things with a range of odors (e.g., perfume, vinegar, soap, cinnamon). Ask them to try to define what they are smelling.
G. With the students' eyes closed again, pass around something to taste (sweet, sour, bitter, smooth) and have them try to define what they are tasting.
H. After the various experiences with the senses, the students

---

Strategy eight was contributed by Mary Dean, Shelby State Community College, Memphis, Tennessee.

should be more in touch with their primary senses and better able to use them in writing.

I.   The class could end with an oral group composition that appeals to *all* the senses. That is, one person begins the paragraph with a phrase, and each succeeding person adds a phrase until the paragraph has several sentences of vivid descriptive material. The sentences may be written on the board as the paragraph is composed.

J.   Now the students are ready to write a descriptive paper, appealing to one or all of the senses. Good literary examples are found in the writings of Thomas Wolfe, D.H. Lawrence, Dylan Thomas, William Carlos Williams, and Wallace Stevens.

Variations

A.   Instead of the oral composition at the end, the students may individually write a descriptive paragraph that appeals to one of the senses concretely and specifically.

B.   Examples of descriptive writing could be used in a later class to illustrate imagery in fiction, poetry, drama, and critical essays.

C.   You might have the students just focus on one or two persons in step D of the process section.

9. "Richard Cory": Writing to an Audience

Group size: Large- or small-group discussion.
Time required: About eighty minutes.
Materials: Each student will need paper and pen or pencil. The literature selection (see step C, process section) may be duplicated for distribution after the exercise is completed.

Goals

A. To help students discover the concept of audience in writing.
B. To help students understand how the language used in writing depends on the audience.
C. To have students write a short assignment addressed to a defined audience.
D. (Optional) To have students share their writing with members of the class.

Process

A. Introduce the concept of writing to a particular audience using your own examples; remind the students how audience fits into the composition model.
B. Explain the goals of this exercise.
C. Read to them the basic data from some famous piece of literature —an outline of the basic facts from "Richard Cory" by Edwin Arlington Robinson, for example. You may want to invent some provocative particulars. Here is what we would tell our class about the poem:

> Richard Cory was in his late fifties. After graduating from Princeton with a liberal arts degree, he inherited a large estate from his father, J. P. Cory, the steel magnate. Cory was well known for his excellent manners and elegant dress. Despite his immense wealth, he never lorded it over the townspeople less fortunate than himself. He could sometimes be seen engaged in conversation with them. Nevertheless, envious glances were often seen coming from the townspeople when he walked by. On July 8, in the morning around nine o'clock, his butler, Peabody P. Priss, discovered Richard Cory's body in Cory's study. He had shot himself in the head.

D. You may want your students to take notes while you read your summary.
E. Once the summary is read and notes taken, give each student one of the following writing tasks to be done in class; somewhere

around twenty to thirty minutes should be enough time to complete any of them. Stress that in writing the assignment they are to choose the appropriate facts and language to fit the audience to whom they are writing; also, they may make up some names and facts to give more substance to their writings for specific purposes and audiences. The writing tasks are as follows:

1. A newspaper account of Cory's death.
2. A letter from Cory's wife to her aged mother.
3. An autopsy report.
4. A society column about the suicide and the funeral.
5. The sheriff's report.
6. A letter from Peabody P. Priss to his friend, High Brow, valet to Senator J. J. Gross III.
7. Make up your own assignment.

F. Once the papers have been written, volunteers may be invited to read their work to the class.
G. After each paper is read, the class may discuss the language appropriateness and the selection of details.
H. At the end of the discussion about writing to an audience, read the poem to the class. Discuss the poet's language and its relation to his particular purpose and audience.

Variations

A. Many stories or poems may be used, e.g., "The Lottery" by Shirley Jackson; "Mr. Flood's Party" by Edwin Arlington Robinson; any of Robert Browning's shorter dramatic monologues; any poem or short story of love, murder, or intrigue.
B. You may want to split students into groups and have them write each of the assignments. Then have one reporter read the group's paper.
C. You may wish to duplicate some of the better papers written by individuals.
D. If you wrote along with your students, you may wish to read your essay to the class.

10.   The Telegram: Form and Audience

Group size: Any size group can do this exercise.
Time required: The time varies depending on the class, but planning for two to four class periods is reasonable.
Materials: Each student needs a copy of the telegram and instructions (samples of both are included at the end of this strategy).

Goals

A. To help the student consider the implications in language choices.
B. To help the student discover that choosing a form influences choices in purpose, material, organization, language, and audience.
C. To help the student discover the diversity resulting when writers beginning with the same material make different decisions about approaching the material.
D. To help the student discover how much he or she knows about using various forms of writing.

Process

A. After reading the telegram, the students discuss the implications of the wording, considering the contrast between the situation, a son's death, and the wording, formal and distant.
B. Then each student receives a set of directions which are read and discussed in class. Students especially ought to discuss issues the writer must consider. For example, two of the approaches specified in the instructions imply very different concerns: a reporter for a small hometown newspaper must consider what the people in small towns expect in their papers, while an officer writing to his superior needs a form for the report.
C. Following the discussion, each student writes.
D. Afterwards, form small groups of students, giving them the same instructions handed out earlier.
E. There are several options for the group work: (1) each group selects one or two papers to read to the class; (2) the students in the group discuss their papers and then rewrite them, using insights from the group experience; or (3) copies of one or two

---

Strategy ten was contributed by Kathy Eisele, Delta College, University Center, Michigan.

papers from each group can be made for later discussion by the class.

Telegram and Instructions

The following telegram can be used for this strategy:

Mr. and Mrs. Frederick E. Kingsley:

The Secretary of the Army has asked me to express his deep regret that your son, Private First Class Thomas E. Kingsley, died in Vietnam on 20 March 1971. He was on a military mission when an automatic explosive device placed by a friendly force detonated. Please accept my deepest sympathy. This confirms personal notification made by a representative of the Secretary of the Army.

Kenneth G. Wickham
Major General USA
The Adjutant General
Department of the Army
Washington, D.C.

The telegram ends an article, "Letters Home," published in the June 1974 issue of *Harper's* magazine. "Letters Home" is a collection of the letters written by Private Kingsley to his parents during his assignment in Vietnam. Having a complete copy of the article is helpful, particularly for background purposes during the discussion, but it is not mandatory.

Each person also needs a copy of one of the following three sets of instructions:

1. First option
   a. Use the information in the telegram to write one or two paragraphs for a small hometown newspaper story reporting the death of a local soldier.
   b. Use the information in the telegram as part of an argument in a speech to gain support for the war.
   c. In each situation, you will have to add other material.

2. Second option
   a. Use the information in the telegram as part of an argument in a speech asking for the end of the war.
   b. Write a report of the incident from the officer in charge to his superior.
   c. In each situation, you will have to add other material.

3. Third option
    a. Use the information in the telegram to write one or two paragraphs for a big city newspaper story reporting the death of a soldier from a nearby town.
    b. Write one or two paragraphs of a short story using this incident.
    c. In each situation, you will have to add other material.

11. Discovering Form in Writing

Group size: Groups of three or four.
Time required: The time varies depending on the class, but planning for parts of two or three class periods is reasonable.
Materials: Each student needs copies of various forms of writing, which can be provided by students or the instructor. Providing some material is helpful at the beginning of the discussion because everyone will then be starting from the same material. Classes have successfully used editorials, front-page newspaper articles, letters to the editor, technical articles, essays, directions, legal documents, material for a child from eight to ten years old, and myths. Selecting a few of these forms has proved more successful than using all of them.

Goals

A. To help the student become aware of a variety of forms in writing.
B. To help the student discover that choices in form, purpose, material, organization, language, and audience are related.
C. To help the student experiment with these choices in his or her own writing.

Process

A. Go over the goals of the exercise.
B. Distribute copies of the written material and give students time to read them.
C. Split into groups, and give students the following instructions: "Each group is to study only one of the forms. [Assign one article for each group to study.] One member should act as a recorder for the group. As a group, study the article assigned to you and decide on answers to the following questions about the form of the article: (1) What is the purpose that the author had in writing this article? (2) Who is the audience? How do you know? (3) Why is the article organized in the manner it is? (4) How does the language, especially word choice, fit the audience? Be sure that you have reasons and examples from the article to support your answers."
D. When the groups are finished answering the questions, have each group's recorder give his or her report to the entire class.

Strategy eleven was contributed by Kathy Eisele, Delta College, University Center, Michigan.

E. Summarize. Point out the relationship between audience, purpose, form, and language.
F. (Optional) You might instruct the class to write their next class assignment using one of the forms studied in class.

Variations

A. You might have the students individually read the chosen materials and answer the questions. Then have a class discussion of the articles.
B. Have the small groups write an article using a form reported on by one of the other groups. Have them use a topic of their own choice.

12. A Long Writing Project

Group size: Small groups of about six students. This exercise is best undertaken after group members have worked together for some period of time; this will allow them to develop some rapport before embarking on a long-range project such as this.
Time required: This depends on the extent of the project planned by the instructor. However, three weeks of class periods might be allocated to this exercise and two class sessions for presentation of the results of the project. Or the instructor may wish to give the groups less in-class time over a period longer than three weeks.
Materials: The groups will need copies of the instructions. (A sample is included at the end of this strategy.)

Goals

A. To encourage students to study in some depth an important topic of interest to them.
B. To help them gather material for an extended composition.
C. To provide a forum for expanding their group skills.
D. To facilitate group members becoming better acquainted.
E. (Optional) To allow students the chance to use other media for communication.

Process

A. A week or so before the groups begin working on the project, pass out the instructions.
B. Discuss the goals of the project.
C. Read through the instructions for the project with your students. Discuss any questions as they arise.
D. Once the instructions have been read and discussed, students will want to know about topics for this project. Here are several suggestions.
    1. Long-range projects may be on some question that has been raised in your class reading and discussion.
    2. All students might be asked to bring to class a list ranking in order of importance the five most difficult problems facing people their age; a list of five topics about which each of them would like to know more; or a list of questions they would like answered if they knew someone who had all the answers. Or just ask them to bring in three topics that would

be good subjects for a project like this. (N.B.: The instructions about finding a topic should be given with the instructions for the whole exercise—a week before work begins on it.)

E. After discussion of the topics for the project, you might wish to give a writing assignment. Many types of writing suggest themselves:

1. A report on the major findings of the study. (You might want to suggest a maximum length.)

2. An opinion essay on the most profitable aspect of the project; taking a position about some issue inherent to the project topic; and so on.

3. An analysis of how the group went about doing the project: how they narrowed down the topic; how they split up the responsibilities; disagreements; how they solved those disagreements; what the group needed to do to improve its functioning.

4. A comparison-contrast of how the group changed over the course of the project or how the end product differed from the goals set.

5. A character sketch of another member of the group or of oneself as perceived functioning in the group.

6. An evaluation of the group that answers questions about group behavior. This could be used to give mutual feedback within each group at the end of the project: What were the main characteristics of the ways we worked together? What did we learn about problems to avoid while working in a task group? What needed work was not done?

7. Free writing after group sessions.

F. On the first day of group meetings about the project, you might give the following suggestions: "You have three weeks to put together your project for presentation and to write your report (or other essay assignment). Spend one or two class periods narrowing down and arriving at a consensus decision about the topic. Next, spend some time dividing up the topic into units of study for individuals or teams from the group. After deciding on the topic and splitting up the work, you will need to decide how to present the results to the class. Keep in mind the directions given. I will circulate among the groups to observe and to help when necessary."

G. At the end of three weeks, time should be allocated for the presentation of the group projects.

H. You may wish to spend one class period letting the groups evaluate their project and the process of the group.

I. N.B.: The benefits of this project are of two types: the content and the process. Students will know more about some topic they have spent time studying. Also, students will have been involved in a very immediate process. They will have discovered a topic and talked about it with a group; discovered like opinions and disagreements about the topic; and figured out ways of communicating their new understanding to the whole class. Therefore, whether the project presentation is creative and challenging or dull and simple, the students can learn a great deal about themselves, others, and the topic. The instructor's main tasks are to encourage the group members and to help the groups solve serious diagreements. Finally, the writing that flows from this exercise can be about the content and/or the process.

Variations

A. The topic of the projects might be generated from one of the earlier consensus decision-making exercises.

B. The projects might be done by individuals, thus eliminating the group process part of the exercise.

Sample Instructions

The following is an example of instructions for a long-range writing project. Remember, you will probably wish to alter the format and wording of the instructions to fit your class needs.

> During the next three weeks, we will, in our groups, create presentations to share with the entire class. Thirty minutes will be allotted for the presentations. Here is a process to use to formulate your presentation.
>
> 1. Decide upon a topic that is agreed upon by consensus: the endeavor of the group project is for your group to explore, share, and expand your experience of some area of life that you all find pertinent to who you are here and now.
>
> 2. Once you have a consensus about the topic to be explored, you will then probably want to divide up the group work. Approach the task on the basis of logic, interest, and feeling.
>
> 3. The group might brainstorm about the topics to be studied by each subgroup to provide focus for them.
>
> 4. Set deadlines for completion of work by subgroups.

5. Brainstorm about and decide upon the methods you will use to present the results of your study. Ideally, your task will be to:
   a. Convince the class that your subject is vital to us.
   b. Involve all members of your group in presenting the subject.
   c. Show some analysis of readings and of information gathered.
   d. Suggest to the class a pattern of action which you outline (as individuals or as a group).
   e. Develop an evaluative instrument for what you have shared with us with which all class members can provide feedback for your group.
6. You may wish to incorporate any or all of the following methods in your presentation: panels, debates, lectures, small-group exercises, chalkboard, posters, films, records, tapes, slides, dialogue, role playing, dramatic interpretations, diagrams, newspaper articles, handout sheets, and readings.
7. Next, you might want to practice your presentation; remember that you have a time limit of thirty minutes; therefore, try to fit in as much of the content of the project as possible.

The group process. There are a few points that you ought to keep in mind about group process:

1. Keep your goals and objectives clear.
2. View differences of opinion as helping, rather than hindering, decision making.
3. Try to use all the resources available to you.
4. Try, as a group, to come up with a method and materials for the presentation which all group members can agree upon and contribute to before and during your presentation.
5. Focus on that part of the topic which most stimulates, interests, and challenges your imagination.
6. Finally, remember that I am available to help you, but that a group of six to eight people is a powerful storehouse of ideas and insights.
7. Listen carefully and with an open mind.
8. Remember that while the end product is important, you need the whole group's participation. So, encourage one another.

The Writing Stage

In the writing stage of the composition process, form or structure becomes a paramount concern, especially the larger rhetorical structure of the paragraph and the overall structure of the essay or writing. Many of the writing decisions, such as audience, purpose, tone, and register, have previously been made in the prewriting stage. Furthermore, most of the main ideas and supporting details have also been generated or discovered in that part of the writing process. What remains is the problem of structuring all those earlier decisions, ideas, and support into an effective, coherent, well-formed writing.

The traditional approach to teaching this forming or structuring stage is to present lectures on formal rhetoric, illustrating them with examples of paragraph and essay development, and to assign professionally written essays for reading and classroom analysis. There is no question that some students have learned from this approach, but there is also no question that many others have *not* learned from it—at least not learned enough to be effective, sophisticated writers. We would not argue that the traditional practices should be abandoned, but they can be modified or supplemented by other strategies to make them more effective and interesting. Lectures on rhetoric, for example, could be made into handouts for class discussion, and groups of students could practice mastering (and teaching to others) one rhetorical skill or structuring principle. Reading should certainly be encouraged—since we obviously learn much about writing from our reading—but using class time for a discussion of the content of professionally written essays is of questionable value for teaching writing.

Fortunately, most students already know much about form and structure. To a great extent, much of what teachers should do in this stage is simply to show them how much rhetoric they already command; we need only raise this subconscious or tacit understanding to a conscious level. We should certainly not assume that all students will know all they need to know about writing structures, but neither should we assume that none of them knows anything. Part of our job as writing teachers is to diagnose students' individual abilities and to implement strategies to help students learn *more* about forming and structuring their ideas in writing.

1. Building Bigger Sentences

Group size: Entire class in a large-group discussion circle.
Time required: No specific limit.
Materials: Writing paper for each student.

Goals

A. To teach students to add more "poundage," concreteness, and vividness to their sentences.
B. To teach students the concept of and the ability to write both mature and complex sentences, and to teach effective sentence style.
C. To teach students the concept of sentence variety as an aid to a better writing style.

Process

A. The instructor explains the goals of the exercise and writes a *very short* sentence on the board. (Some samples are included at the end of this strategy.)
B. Everyone, including the instructor, attempts to expand the sentence into the longest possible sentence without making it awkward or unclear. (The instructor should be forewarned that his or her sentence will not always be the best one.)
C. Volunteers (or everyone) read their sentences and the class discusses them.
D. A new short sentence may be put on the board, and the process may be repeated.
E. The instructor should tell the class that long sentences are not always good sentences, that sentence variety and balance are the ideal.
F. The instructor points out that all the students are capable of writing long, vivid, and complex sentences.

Variations

A. The instructor brings in a series of short, choppy sentences, and the class works on combining these into longer, more complex units.

Strategy one was suggested by the work of Francis Christensen, especially his *Notes Toward a New Rhetoric: Six Essays for Teachers* (New York: Harper and Row, 1967).

B. In small groups students may take their long sentences and combine them into a paragraph on the subject of the sentences.
C. The class members may be instructed to take their long sentences and split them into sentences of varying lengths, then form these sentences into an effective paragraph.
D. The instructor brings in examples of very long sentences, and the class works on cutting unnecessary words from them. (Perhaps some sentences from Henry James would be fun to work with.)

Sample Sentences

The following are examples of very short sentences which might be used for this exercise. Considerably longer and more detailed versions follow each.

1. I left the party and walked home.

   Rewritten version: Leaving the noisy, crowded, smoke-filled room where the party was reaching a crescendo of dirty jokes and raucous laughter, I walked home slowly through the humid April night, smelling the fragrances of tender, recently born spring flowers and sensing the inescapable conclusion that something new, exciting, and important was about to happen in my life.

2. Jones was a short, fat man.

   Rewritten version: Since he stood only slightly over five feet in height, Jones presented an almost comical appearance, with his 230 pounds of flesh collected largely around his waist and pushing forward from his midriff like the ponderous swell of an expectant mother.

3. A trout took the baited hook immediately.

   Rewritten version: As soon as the baited hook had struck the water, a large, speckled trout hit it with tremendous force, splitting the water with its glistening body and diving, with great power, into the deepest, darkest part of the river.

2. Working with Long and Simple Sentences

Group size: Groups of three.
Time required: One class meeting.
Materials: Duplicated copies of long sentences and simple sentences. (Samples are included at the end of this strategy.)

Goals

A. To help students control the length of their sentences.
B. To encourage students to collaborate on a task involving language choices.

Process

A. Discuss the goals of the exercise.
B. Split the class into small groups.
C. Pass out the duplicated materials.
D. With the wordy or just long sentences, tell them to split the sentences into shorter ones while maintaining the same meaning of the passage. You might want to give each group two or three sentences different from those of the other groups, thus shortening the process and covering more sentences.
E. After each group has finished, have the sentences read to the class or written on the board.
F. Discuss the sentence changes. Here are some questions that might be used:
   1. Does the revised group of sentences communicate the same message as the one long sentence?
   2. What effect does shortening the long sentence have on you as a reader?
   3. Should this sentence have been chopped up into smaller units?
G. After this discussion, have the groups re-form; instruct them to take the paragraphs composed of simple sentences and rework them, providing transitional expressions and coupling of sentences where needed for variety.
H. When the groups are finished, have the sentences read in class or written on the board.
I. Discuss the rewritten paragraph using questions similar to those given in step F.

Variations

A. Have students select one or more paragraphs from one of their own essays. Have them write the paragraph in simple sentences; then have them rewrite it in complex or compound sentences. Compare the results. Next, students might rewrite the paragraph by varying the sentences. Have the students get feedback about the revisions from group members.
B. Use a literary source for examples of long sentences (Faulkner, Conrad, James) or short sentences (Hemingway). Have students shorten or lengthen the sentences. Discuss the effects of doing so.

Sample Sentences

The sentences below, taken from student writing, can be used for the sentence-splitting exercise described in this strategy.

> The ancient art of fly-catching is a complex art which requires much, if not more skill and training than is necessary to play well a musical instrument because it takes a great deal of practice to reach the level at which sureness of oneself is attained resulting in sacrificing much of your spare time if you wish to attain any sort of pleasure from the art, intense desire such as this is necessary.

> In the course of our lives, we often hear the phrase, "Cleanliness is next to godliness," and of course, cleanliness would be next to impossible if it were not for soap of which nearly three billion pounds are produced yearly in the United States.

> There is a road I travel every time I go to school that is a secluded street, jutting off of the hustle and bustle of Highland Avenue, and as soon as I turn on it, I can sense the relaxation around it: the aura of precision and order that comes from its well-kept lawns.

The essay below has been rewritten using only simple sentences. Students can rework it according to the directions for this strategy.

> It was Saturday morning at 10:30. I opened my eyes. The world was gray and dreary. It was raining. Two hours earlier, another young man had risen. He slept on the cold floor of a run-down project. I laid in bed. I had thoughts of the night before. They rushed pleasantly through my mind. The young hoodlum awoke. He went into the streets. He had a hangover from the cheap wine from the previous night.
> I had waffles smothered in syrup for breakfast. I read the morning paper. I looked at the box scores. Later, I watched the

football game on my color TV. I called some friends. I wanted to make sure they were all going to the party that night. At the same time, the young man sat outside a corner grocery. He munched on a stolen apple. Soon, his gang had gathered. They began to talk of a plan. They wanted to make some easy money. The young man was no chicken. He was ready to prove it. He would go along with the plan.

At 9:30 that night, the party began to pick up. Some of the kids were getting drunk. Some were dancing their heads off. Some were getting into the music. Perhaps I too would get up and dance after a few more drinks. The rain fell on the youth's hair. It ran down his neck. He entered the liquor store. He shivered with both fear and cold. Quickly, he pulled the gun. He ordered the money from the storekeeper. He turned to run out the door. He heard three blasts from a shotgun call his name.

3. Jumbled Sentences: Finding Paragraph Structure

Group size: This exercise can be used in either a large-group or small-group setting.
Time required: Approximately one hour.
Materials: Copies of paragraphs which have been "jumbled" in sentence order. (Samples are included at the end of this strategy.)

Goals

A. To show students their tacit understanding of paragraph structure and development.
B. To encourage attention to and systematic analysis of rhetorical structure.
C. To encourage student participation in class.

Process

A. The instructor explains the goals of the activity and distributes copies of the exercise to all students.
B. The instructor explains that the sentences in each paragraph have been jumbled and the students are to place the sentences in their correct order. (To save time, students can merely list the correct sequence by number, rather than writing out the sentences.)
C. The instructor asks students to write down "clues" which they used to put the sentences in order. How did they choose the lead sentences, and how did they know which sentence followed the first one?
D. Students could work on these paragraphs individually or in small groups. The small-group structure works best with this exercise since the paragraphs stimulate much student discussion, with the students in each group working towards a consensus on the placement of each sentence.
E. Once the groups have reached agreement on the sequence of sentences, the entire class can discuss the "clues" used to perceive sentence order in a paragraph.

Sample Sentences

The three examples that follow are arranged according to their degree of difficulty, from the easiest to the most difficult. Although the exercise should challenge students, the instructor should not use a paragraph which would only frustrate class members. The directions for the exercise are to rearrange each set of sentences so that they form clear, unified paragraphs.

1. Either you throw everything into a suitcase, burdening yourself with unnecessary clothes, or you pack so sparingly you don't have enough variety.

2. You don't have to make either mistake if you think through the kind of vacation you're likely to be doing most.

3. We've pulled together a list of basic clothes plus some tips, and if you plan well you should wear everything and not feel bored.

4. If you're like most travelers, you make one of two mistakes when you pack.

1. Beneath them lies another group: the one-third of black America that struggles by on less than $4,500 a year and makes up the troubled underclass.

2. Almost one-third have family incomes of $10,000 or more and enjoy many of the amenities of middle-class status.

3. In recent years the underclass has made some economic and social gains, but its progress has been fitful.

4. Indeed, the nation's 24 million blacks are split into three groups of roughly equal size.

5. Although some black Americans have "made it" in our white-dominated society, anybody who looks at a slum knows that not all blacks have made impressive economic and social advances, that huge numbers are weighted down by weariness and desolation.

6. Another one-third, earning between $4,500 and $10,000, are either on the lower edges of the middle class or stand a fair chance of lifting themselves into it.

1. Most modern classifications begin with three great divisions or zones ranging from immature to mature soils.

2. They may be classified on the basis on texture (size of particles) as clayey, silty, or sandy.

3. Three examples of well-developed soils are the tropical red soils, the northern forest soils, and the grassland soils.

4. Soils may be classified in a half-dozen ways, according to various properties.

5. Other classifications have been based on color, parent material, type of crop raised, and many other bases.

however, many students argue that sentence three doesn't belong in the paragraph, since its subject is soils, not classification of soils.)

4. Jumbled Paragraphs: Finding Essay Structure

Group size: This exercise could be used in either a large-group or small-group setting.
Time required: Approximately one hour.
Materials: Copies of essays which have been "jumbled" in paragraph order. (A sample is included at the end of this strategy.)

Goals

A. To show students their tacit understanding of essay structure and development.
B. To encourage attention to and systematic analysis of rhetorical structure.
C. To encourage student participation in class.

Process

A. The instructor explains the goals of the activity and distributes copies of the exercise to all students.
B. The instructor explains that the paragraphs in the essay have been jumbled and the students are to place the paragraphs in their correct order. (For more difficult versions of this exercise, see the variations section.)
C. The instructor asks students to write down "clues" which they used to put the paragraphs in order. How did they choose the introductory paragraph, the sequence of the middle paragraphs, and the concluding paragraph?
D. Students could work on these essays individually or in small groups. The small-group structure works best since the exercise stimulates much student discussion as they reach a consensus on the placement of each paragraph.
E. Once the groups have reached agreement on the sequence of paragraphs, the entire class can discuss the "clues" used to determine the paragraph order of the essay.

Variations

A. Instead of "jumbling" the order of the paragraphs in the essay, the instructor can obliterate all paragraph markers (making the essay one long paragraph) and ask students to reach a consensus on the points where paragraphs should begin.
B. The instructor could both obliterate paragraph markers *and* jumble some of the paragraphs in the essay. This variation,

however, should be designed carefully and used only with a fairly sophisticated, confident group of students.

Sample Essay

The paragraphs of the following essay have been jumbled. The correct order of paragraphs is 5, 2, 7, 3, 6, 1, 8, 4. The essay was written by Ed Roach, a student at D.S. Lancaster Community College, Clifton Forge, Virginia.

The Causes of the Civil War

[1] The South, after hearing Lincoln's proposal on slavery, felt that its rights had been violated. The southern leaders decided that their states should be allowed to retain many soverign rights not already designated to the federal government under the Constitution of 1776, including the right for any state to secede from the Union if it felt its rights had been impaired. The North, on the other hand, agreed with Lincoln's decision, knowing that with national growth slavery would soon be diminished and would no longer be an issue of importance.

[2] In 1851–52, Harriet Beecher Stowe published a novel entitled *Uncle Tom's Cabin*. This novel was the story of a Negro family's treatment and bondage. The book, therefore, infuriated both the North and the South, but for different reasons. The North, which was almost totally against slavery, could not believe that such things actually happened and cried out for the immediate abolishment of slavery. The South, on the other hand, felt that the slaves were its property and that the North had no right interfering. The South felt that the book was a misrepresentation of fact.

[3] Instead of this decision, the court chose to try the case and then ruled that (1) Scott remain a slave under Missouri law; (2) Negros of slave descent were "inferior" and could not sue in federal court; and (3) the Missouri Compromise, which had prohibited slavery in free territory, was unconstitutional. This decision by the court was a political bombshell and widened the gap between the North and the South even further.

[4] In summary, the printing of *Uncle Tom's Cabin*, the Dred Scott Decision, the election of Lincoln, and the issue of state rights were the four things which triggered the War Between the States, which began as a "romantic adventure" and ended as a bitter conflict. In this war, brother fought brother, and father fought son, often splitting entire households. This war raged for over four years as the most bloody act of vengeance in the history of the United States, ending in freedom and equality for all men and leaving a bitterness between the North and South which has lasted for more than a century and remains a separating issue today.

[5] The decade preceding the Civil War was one of bitter strife and conflict. The North and South were involved in a debate

over the issue of slavery. The South, which depended on slavery for both economic and domestic reasons, felt that it had the right to maintain slavery and was ready to fight should this right be challenged. Slavery, however, served no purpose to the North; therefore, it felt that the keeping of humans as work animals was entirely wrong and that slavery should be abolished. Slavery, therefore, was the overriding issue which led up to the Civil War. But there were four main causes (all of them converging on the single issue of slavery) which actually triggered the start of the Civil War: the printing of *Uncle Tom's Cabin*, the Dred Scott Decision, the election of Abraham Lincoln to the presidency, and the issue of state rights.

[6] After the 1860 election of Abraham Lincoln as President of the United States, the South felt that it was at a great disadvantage because of Lincoln's views on slavery. Lincoln proposed that the South should be allowed to keep its slaves but that any new state or territory added to the United States should not be permitted to have slaves. The South, however, felt that this put it in an inferior position in Congress, where most of its battles had been won. With the addition of new states and territories to the Union, Congress would grow, and the South felt that its ability to keep Congress under control would be lost and eventually, so would its rights to slavery.

[7] The second factor leading up to the Civil War, the Dred Scott Decision, was a decision of the Supreme Court of the United States regarding the status of slavery in the territories. Dred Scott was a Negro slave who belonged to a doctor. The doctor took his slave to free territory and resided there for some time. The doctor then returned, with his slave, to slave territory. After the death of the doctor, the abolitionists persuaded Dred Scott to sue for his freedom. The Missouri Supreme Court ruled that Scott was not entitled to his freedom. Scott then carried his case on to the United States Supreme Court, where it could simply have been ruled that Scott was not a citizen of the United States and, therefore, could not sue in court.

[8] This issue of states rights, therefore, was the singlemost main cause of the Civil War. The South was determined to claim all within its boundaries as its property after seceding. Since the South did not wish to have a federal fort in its midst and the North did not wish to give up what it felt belonged to the Union, the first shots were fired at Fort Sumter in Charleston Harbour, South Carolina, on April 11, 1861.

5. A Group Approach to Thesis Statements and Topic Sentences

Group size: Groups of three to six students.
Time required: One or two class periods depending on variations added.
Materials: Duplicated copies of the generalization(s) and jumbled topic sentences or data if also used in the exercise. (Samples are included at the end of this strategy.)

Goals

A. To help students learn how to write topic sentences and thesis statements.
B. To facilitate the working together of students on a common task.
C. To help students avoid unsupported generalizations.

Process

A. Discuss the goals of the exercise with the class.
B. Hand out copies of the duplicated material.
C. Split the class into small groups.
D. Read and answer questions about the following directions: "Writing clear thesis statements is a necessary skill for any writer. A thesis statement summarizes the main points of an essay, thereby giving the paper a focus. Also important are topic sentences at the beginning of each paragraph. They give a paper coherence because they provide a lead-in to the next point to be discussed in the paper. A thesis statement and topic sentences are the skeleton upon which are added the reasons, examples, and explanations that are the musculature of the essay. On the worksheet that was passed out is a general statement that should be made into a manageable thesis statement by breaking it down into elements which can be discussed in an essay. Once your group has written a thesis statement, each group member should write a topic sentence introducing one of the topics mentioned in the thesis. When all groups members are finished writing the topic sentences, the group should order them, thus forming an outline for a paper. These thesis statements and topic sentences will be shared with the rest of the class. You have about twenty minutes to complete this part of the exercise."
E. When the groups have completed their work, they may either read their thesis statements and topic sentences or write them on the board. They can also be duplicated for the next class meeting.

F. Students can discuss each group's work. Here are some possible questions:
    1. Does the thesis statement narrow down the generalization to a manageable form for an essay?
    2. Does the thesis summarize the main points mentioned in the topic sentences?
    3. Do the topic sentences all relate directly to the points mentioned in the thesis?
    4. Is the order of the topic sentences logical?
    5. Questions of your own.

Variations

A. There are many other activities that might be needed to help students learn about topic sentences and thesis statements. If your students need more work on thesis skills, this variation and the ones that follow may be useful. For this variation, give groups a list of topic sentences. From these, they should formulate a thesis statement that summarizes the material in the topic sentences. Thesis statements can then be read by a recorder from each group. Possible sources for topic sentences are selections from the class text that the students have not yet read; a student essay that was particularly well organized; any well-written essay (the essay might be distributed to students after they have written their thesis statements so that they can compare); or sentences written by the instructor that pertain to some topic the class has been studying.
B. Taking variation A one step further, you might jumble several topic sentences. (A sample is included at the end of this strategy.) Have students put them in logical order and then write the thesis. If you do this, make sure that there is some order implied in the topic sentences. Also, you might ask the group to give reasons why they ordered the topic sentences the way they did.
C. You might introduce strategy five by giving the students an essay which rambles because it does not have a clear thesis statement and topic sentences.
D. If you use topic sentences or a generalization related to an essay from a text students will be reading, you might discuss the essay immediately after this exercise so that they can compare their work with the original.
E. Another approach to this process would be to give students paragraphs without topic sentences. Then have them write topic sentences. (A sample is included at the end of this strategy.)

F. Give groups data or examples randomly listed. Have them order
    the data into several categories, write topic sentences for each
    cluster of data, and write a thesis statement. Then the group can
    write an essay from the thesis, topic sentences, and data. Again,
    the source of the data might be an essay from a class text.
G. If you wish to discuss paragraph endings, give students an essay
    without ending sentences for the paragraphs. Instruct the groups
    to write appropriate ending sentences that summarize the para-
    graphs.
H. To discuss final paragraphs for essays, you might pass out copies
    of an essay with the last paragraph deleted. Have groups write
    summary statements. Or have the groups add end paragraphs to
    any of the essays that result from the activities listed in this
    section.
I. Give students a summary or ending statement of an essay. Have
    them write a thesis statement that includes all the ideas in the
    ending, and then instruct them to write fitting topic sentences
    flowing out of the ending.

Sample Exercises

As discussed in the strategy, generalizations like the following can be
distributed to groups to be broken down into workable thesis
statements and then topic sentences.

> Air pollution affects all of us.
>
> The cafeteria needs improvement.
>
> This school needs more electives.
>
> Today was terrible (wonderful).
>
> Most people are unconcerned about the problems of other
> people.
>
> Christmas is a mess.
>
> Noise has bad effects on people.
>
> Most people are conformists.

The following is an example of a set of jumbled topic sentences
that could be used for variation B.

> The next problem with air pollution is the destruction of the
> ozone layer around the earth.
>
> Plants are affected by air pollution.

Another problem affecting us is the smog created by exhaust emissions.

Our bodies are harmed by air pollutants.

The two essays below, both of which were written by students, may be used for variation E, where students are to supply topic sentences. These samples might also be used in other ways. For instance, leave out the ending paragraph and have the students write one; omit the thesis statement and have students write one; or jumble the data from an essay and have the students order it.

Many times when we hear the word "amateur," thoughts of someone who really doesn't know much invade our minds. Amateur has not always suggested someone who didn't know what he or she was doing. The word "amateur" comes from the Latin word "amator," which means lover. "Amateur" originally meant someone who had a special interest in a field without being a professional in that certain field. The opinions and observations of these "lovers of art and knowledge" were respected. Today, we tend to only listen to the opinions of those who have advanced knowledge or special training in that field. However, many so-called "amateurs" have led the way to greater knowledge in several fields. One of the fields that amateurs have excelled in is science.

_____ .

Franklin was a prominent politician, newspaper publisher, print-er, and writer. He was one of the men who drafted the Declaration of Independence in 1776. Later, he also played a big role in gaining the support of France for the colonies during the American Revolution. Benjamin Franklin was without formal training in science. Yet, he made several important discoveries about electricity. He was also the first person to make a scientific study of the Gulf Stream.

_____ .

His career as a candy-seller came to a sudden halt when the conductor found young Edison making nitroglycerin in the baggage car of the train. Nitroglycerin is a highly explosive substance that can be set off by a sharp jolt—and sharp jolts often occurred on country railroads during the 1850's. Edison eventually became one of America's most famous inventors. He discovered the "Edison effect"—a heated metal gives off electrons. This effect, known as thermo-electricity, is being studied as a way to produce electricity for special uses.

_____ .

They began their careers as bicycle repairmen in Dayton, Ohio. Later, they manufactured their own bicycles and had a profitable small business going. The Wright Brothers were also interested in aeronautics. As amateurs, they followed the gliding demonstrations reported in newspapers and scientific journals. In time, they began designing and building their own gliders. During their experiments, they proved that many of the known facts about gliding and aerodynamics were wrong. On the basis of their own experiments, they found better theories. Still amateurs, they designed and built the first successful, engine-powered aircraft, thus becoming the initiators of the airplane industry.

All of these men, classified as "amateurs" by our present-day definition, made astounding discoveries and inventions. Today, we should think twice before we look down on amateurs—they may know more than we think.

Colors have a marked effect on human emotions. Color, whether on an artist's canvas or in the clothes a person wears, add intensity, variety and appeal. However, this does not universally apply in the same way to every hue in the spectrum. Just as each color is different, so is the feeling it evokes.

_____ .

This idea is seen evident by black being connected with mourning; grey is often associated with a threat or premonition of more darkness to come. When these colors are mixed with a contrast such as white or cream, they take on a mysterious, haunting aura. The contrast can be in different shapes or in forms such as crystal moonlight piercing a grey night, or the creamy expanse of a woman's skin against the neckline of a black dress.

_____ .

Purple has an earthy, regal nature. King's vestments are often a deep purple, and erotic items of apparel are quite often this shade. Wine, which affects one's mood to the more romantic lazy side, is often a deep purple-red, and much of its enjoyment stems from the appreciation of its color.

_____ .

This is especially true of red. It has long represented anger, or potential danger. In spite of this hidden explosive factor, it is a highly desirable shade. How often has the cliche "a woman in a red dress" stirred up feelings of the forbidden and of excitement because it is a taboo? Always in cartoons, dynamite is shown as little red sticks. Who would dare paint them green?

_____ .

Light shades, pastels, are very restful. They are not distracting. That is why many schools paint the walls light green or blue. It is providing a calm atmosphere for study and reflection.

The Postwriting Stage

The postwriting stage can be broken into two parts: editing and proofreading. In many ways the editing process is an extension of the writing stage—it is a matter of taking a fresh, critical look at one's writing, bringing to bear all the intuition, knowledge, and understanding one has of writing processes and forms, in order to be sure that the written product says or is what the writer wants it to say or be. In the sense that it is a part of the process that deals with the finished product, however, editing belongs in this postwriting stage.

We have found it useful to teach editing as a postwriting process, as a separate process to be done when the first draft of a writing is completed. At this stage, the writer takes a cool, objective look at his or her writing to see if it really speaks to the audience and purpose he or she has in mind; if it has the correct tone and register he or she had hoped for; if it is rhetorically structured for maximum effect; and if the diction and syntax of the sentences are precise and smooth. In this editing process, then, the writer is looking for *major* problems in his or her writing.

The proofreading part of the postwriting stage is the final step of the writing process. It is to writing what table etiquette is to eating. In this final proofreading process, the writer looks for minor flaws in writing, flaws at the sentence level: spelling, subject-verb agreement, verb tense consistency, dialect features, and so on. It is an important part of the writing process, and, fortunately, one in which the writer can receive much help from others. In stressing the importance of the postwriting stage, it might also be pointed out to students that professional writers receive much help from others—colleagues, professional editors, and professional proofreaders—at this point.

The postwriting process that we have briefly outlined here is not new. However, the discussion of spelling, punctuation, and syntax correction has been clouded with controversy for some time. The approach of prescriptive grammarians dominated for many years. More recently, with the findings of linguists such as Labov, Chomsky, Linneberg, and others, many assumptions about prescriptive grammar have been called into question. Also, the increased understanding about the relationship between dialect differences and the teaching of language has added new complexities to the approaches teachers must now take in "correcting" students' language (see *Students' Right to Their Own Language* [Urbana, Ill.: National Council of Teachers of English, 1974]). In attempting to alter patterns of student language, a teacher is tampering with the psychosocial life of the student. Consequently, we recognize that a short introduction to postwriting like this one needs to be coupled with serious study of language, composition, and correction.

For our purposes here, it is essential that the composition teacher acknowledge that the postwriting process deals primarily with surface features of the language system. If a teacher places too great an emphasis on editing and proofreading at the outset of a composition course, the language, ideas, and experiences a student must start with in the composition process will be overshadowed by the student's fear of error. Mina Shaughnessey concludes in *Errors and Expectations* (New York: Oxford University Press, 1977) that "if a writer is not worried about being wrong, if he sees a chance for repairing and perfecting his copy at a later point before anyone sees it, he will be free to think about what he means and not worry so much about the way he is saying things, a worry that almost inevitably cuts him off from his grammatical intuitions. Furthermore, by withholding closure on his sentences, he is more likely to work on them and, in the process, begin to be aware of his power to make choices (semantic and organizational) that bring him closer and closer to his intended meaning" (pp. 79–80). Editing and proofreading should therefore be taught as the last step in the composition process.

Last position in the process does not imply last in importance. Confusing sentence structure, spelling problems, and inaccurate punctuation are hindrances to one's reader. Student writers thus need to gain control of syntax, spelling, and punctuation to communicate effectively. Development of prewriting and writing skills will lead to fewer postwriting problems, but students still need consistent help in this area. The help given on syntax, punctuation, and spelling must be preceded by careful diagnosis. Shaughnessey's *Errors and Expectations* is an excellent guide through ways of diagnosing and approaching student problems in the postwriting stage. "Errors" need to be seen as part of a highly organized structure of each person's language. Therefore, to be really effective in helping students gain mastery of the written mode, teachers need a well-developed understanding of language. The following exercises should help composition teachers with editing and proofreading instruction, but much work must be done on the basis of individual needs.

1. Peer Essay Reading

Group size: Depends on the number of students you wish to have read other students' papers. We suggest that triads or pairs are the most practical size.
Time required: Again, this depends on the size of the groups, but twenty-five to thirty-five minutes should be sufficient for triads; less time is needed for pairs.
Materials: A copy of the instructions and student essays. (Sample instructions are included at the end of this strategy.)

Goals

A. To allow students to receive feedback about their writing from their peers.
B. To let students experience other students' essays.
C. To help students to learn about criticizing and proofreading.
D. To allow students to receive help on their essays before they are turned in to the teacher.
E. To encourage good rapport among class members.
F. To expand the students' sense of audience.

Process

A. Discuss the goals of this strategy. (We suggest that this exercise be used only after the students have been meeting together for a time sufficient for them to feel comfortable with each other.)
B. Split into groups of two or three members. (Students might be allowed to select the members of their group or pair. These groupings might remain the same throughout the rest of the course or they may change.)
C. Carefully read through the instructions the first time you use this strategy with a class, and remind them of the instructions before subsequent uses.
D. Discuss the instructions.
E. The students complete the exercise in their groups.

Variations

A. This exercise can be done in larger groups if the students have a well-developed sense of trust in each other.
B. You may let the students revise their essays if they wish after this exercise and turn them in at the next class meeting.

Sample Instructions

The instructions that follow are designed to prepare a class for the peer essay sharing described in this strategy. However, they can be modified to include the following variations. Members of the dyads can outline on paper each other's essay structure, pointing out the thesis or main point and specifying how that point was developed or substantiated. Or, in triads, one student can act as editor and one as proofreader.

> The task for today is to read closely the papers of class members; to both give and receive feedback on the papers; and (optional) to ask for any areas that the reader of your paper could suggest for improving the written communication. The steps are as follows.
>
> 1. Read each other's paper carefully.
> 2. Without looking at the paper, tell the author what you think he or she is saying, or, if it is a narrative, tell the story back to the author as precisely as you can.
> 3. Then your partner(s) should give you the same type of feedback on your paper.
> 4. After this, if you want to ask your partner(s) about anything which seems unclear, you may do so; if you wish to ask for constructive suggestions, you may. You might want to ask for such information as:
>   a. Was there any place in my story that was hard to follow? (narrative)
>   b. Is there any point that you just did not really understand?
>   c. Was there any place in which my examples, reasons, or explanation needed developing?
>   d. Was there any place where I should add more details to my description?
>   e. Is there any place where I seemed to wander from my topic?
>   f. Were there any transitions that were unclear or missing?
>   g. Anything else that you want feedback on: spelling, sentence fragments, run-on sentences, punctuation, sentence variety, style, etc.
> 5. After each of you has given and received feedback on the essays, you may decide to rework your essay. If so, you may turn it in at the next class meeting; if not, turn in your essay at the end of class. Remember that good feedback is specific, not general. Constructive: "I think that this sentence could be more clear if you added some color words in your description of the trees." Destructive: "Your sentences are lousy." Also remember to check with your group members

to make sure your comments are clear. The attitudes which make this sharing helpful are (a) mutual trust; (b) recognition that the helping situation is a joint situation of trust; (c) a real listening to each other; (d) a mutual recognition that whatever is said is merely how we subjectively see things and not necessarily the absolute, objective truth; and (e) a mutual recognition that we want to communicate effectively and that to do this we need reaction from others.

2. The Ties That Bind: Discovering Coherence

Group size: This exercise may be used in either a large-group or small-group setting.
Time required: One to two hours, depending on how many exercises are used and how long they are.
Materials: An essay in which some cohering words and phrases have been deleted. (A sample is included at the end of this strategy.)

Goals

A. To show students their tacit understanding of coherence.
B. To encourage students to closely analyze the text of an essay.
C. To encourage student participation and interaction in the classroom.

Process

A. In their work on cohesion (*Cohesion in English,* New York: Longman, 1976), Halliday and Hasan contend that although there is a structural requirement for a sentence, there is no structural requirement between sentences of a text; hence, a text is held together substantively and by cohesion. Cohesion is that tacitly understood but seldom analyzed quality which "ties together" the sentences of a given text into a unified whole. Halliday and Hasan identify different types of cohesion, including reference, substitution, ellipsis, conjunction (four types: additive—*and, or, nor;* adversative—*yet, although, but;* causal—*so, because;* temporal—*then*), and lexical cohesion. While learning new terminology for classifying cohering words and phrases may not be of much benefit for the composition class, discovering and discussing cohesive words and phrases of a text may help students to perceive coherence, that magical quality which helps to make a text into a unified, organic whole.
B. The instructor should precede this exercise with a short lecture on coherence and unity, pointing out examples of words and phrases often used to achieve cohesion in a text.
C. The instructor distributes copies of an essay in which many cohering words and phrases have been deleted.
D. The instructor asks students to come to a consensus (if they are working in small groups) of the best choices for the deleted

words and to list clues which led the group to the final choice for
each.

E. The groups report to the entire class, discussing any disagreements in choices as they proceed, and the entire class tries for a
consensus of opinion.

Variations

A. As a home assignment, the instructor can ask students to choose
a written text of their choice and to point out the cohering words
and phrases in the text.

B. Also as a home assignment, the instructor can ask students to
create an exercise for other members of the class or group.

C. Instead of deleting cohering words and phrases in a text, the
instructor can ask students to point out the cohering words and
phrases and to explain how they add cohesion to the text.

Sample Essay

Cohering words and phrases have been eliminated from the following essay, written by Ed Roach, a student at D.S. Lancaster Community College, Clifton Forge, Virginia. A key to the deleted words
and phrases follows the essay.

The Causes of the Civil War

The decade preceding the Civil War was __1__ of bitter strife
__2__ conflict. The North __3__ South were involved in a
debate over the issue of slavery. The South, __4__ depended on
__5__ for both economic and domestic reasons, felt that __6__
had the right to maintain slavery and was ready to fight should
this __7__ be challenged. Slavery, __8__, served no purpose to
the North; therefore, __9__ felt that the keeping of humans
as work animals was entirely wrong and that slavery should be
abolished. Slavery, __10__, was the overriding issue which led
up to the Civil War. But there were four main causes (__11__ of
them converging on the single issue of slavery) which actually
triggered the start of the Civil War: the printing of *Uncle Tom's
Cabin*, the Dred Scott Decision, the election of Abraham Lincoln
to the presidency, __12__ the issue of state rights.

In 1851–52, Harriet Beecher Stowe published a __13__ entitled
Uncle Tom's Cabin. This novel was the story of a Negro family's
treatment and bondage. The book, therefore, infuriated both the
North and the South, __14__ for different reasons. The North,
__15__ was almost totally against slavery, could not believe that
such things actually happened and cried out for the immediate

abolishment of __16__. The South, _____ __17__ _____ _____, felt that the slaves were its property and that the North had no right interfering. The South felt that the book was a misrepresentation of fact.

The second __18__ leading up to the Civil War, the Dred Scott Decision, was a decision of the Supreme Court of the United States regarding the status of slavery in the territories. Dred Scott was a Negro slave __19__ belonged to a doctor. The __20__ took his slave to free territory and resided __21__ for some time. The __22__ then returned, with his __23__, to slave territory. After the death of the __24__, the abolitionists persuaded Dred Scott to sue for __25__ freedom on the grounds of having lived in free territory. The Missouri Supreme Court ruled that __26__ was not entitled to his freedom. __27__ then carried his case on to the United States Supreme Court, where it could simply have been ruled that __28__ was not a citizen of the United States and, therefore, could not sue in court.

Instead of this decision, the __29__ chose to try the case __30__ then ruled that (1) __31__ remain a slave under Missouri law; (2) Negros of slave descent were "inferior" and could not sue in federal court; and (3) the Missouri Compromise, __32__ had prohibited slavery in free territory, was unconstitutional. This decision by the court was a political bombshell __33__ widened the gap between the North and the South even further.

After the 1860 election of Abraham Lincoln as President of the United States, the South felt that __34__ was at a great disadvantage because of Lincoln's views on slavery. __35__ proposed that the South should be allowed to keep __36__ slaves __37__ that any new state or territory added to the United States should not be permitted to have __38__. The South, __39__, felt that this put __40__ in an inferior position in Congress, __41__ most of its battles had been won. With the addition of new states __42__ territories to the Union, Congress would grow, and the South felt that __43__ ability to keep Congress under control would be lost and eventually, so would __44__ rights to slavery.

The South, after hearing __45__ proposal on slavery, felt that __46__ rights had been violated. The southern leaders decided that __47__ states should be allowed to retain many soverign rights not already designated to the federal government under the Constitution of 1776, including the __48__ for any state to secede from the Union __49__ it felt its rights had been impaired. The North, _____ __50__ _____ _____, agreed with Lincoln's decision, knowing that with national growth slavery would soon be diminished __51__ would no longer be an issue of importance.

This issue of states rights, therefore, was the singlemost main __52__ of the Civil War. The South was determined to claim all within __53__ boundaries as __54__ property after seceding.

Since the South did not wish to have a federal fort in __55__ midst __56__ the North did not wish to give up what __57__ felt belonged to the Union, the first shots were fired at Fort Sumter in Charleston Harbour, South Carolina, on April 11, 1861.

In summary, the printing of *Uncle Tom's Cabin*, the Dred Scott Decision, the election of Lincoln, and the issue of state rights were the four things which triggered the War Between the States, which began as a "romantic adventure" __58__ ended as a bitter conflict. In this __59__, brother fought brother, and father fought son, often splitting entire households. This __60__ raged for over four years as the most bloody act of vengeance in the history of the United States, ending in freedom __61__ equality for all men __62__ leaving a bitterness between the North and South which has lasted for more than a century and remains a separating issue today.

Key to Deleted Words and Phrases

1. was
2. and
3. and
4. which
5. slavery
6. it
7. right
8. however
9. it
10. therefore
11. all
12. and
13. novel
14. but
15. which
16. slavery
17. on the other hand
18. cause
19. who
20. doctor
21. there

22. doctor
23. slave
24. doctor
25. his
26. Scott
27. Scott
28. he
29. Court
30. and
31. Scott
32. which
33. and
34. it
35. Lincoln
36. its
37. and
38. slaves
39. however
40. it
41. where
42. and

43. its
44. its
45. Lincoln's
46. its
47. their
48. right
49. if
50. on the other hand
51. and
52. cause
53. its
54. its
55. its
56. and
57. it
58. and
59. war
60. conflict
61. and
62. and

3. Dilly Day: Teaching Style

Group size: Entire class in large-group discussion setting.
Time required: No specific limit.
Materials: Paper for each student; the "dilly sentences" may be duplicated and one sheet given to each student. (Sample sentences are included at the end of this strategy.)

Goals

A. To introduce the concepts of sentence style and effectiveness.
B. To encourage students to edit their own writings for effective sentence structure.
C. To encourage class participation and discussion.

Process

A. The instructor collects awkward, confusing, convoluted, or otherwise ineffective sentences from student writings over a period of time (without names of course).
B. The instructor explains the goals of the exercise and writes one of the "dilly" sentences on the board.
C. Everyone, including the instructor, attempts to rewrite the sentence so that it will be clear, smooth, and effective, *while neither deleting nor adding information.* (The instructor should be forewarned that his or her rewrites will not always be the best.)
D. Students should be encouraged to try writing the sentence in various ways until it seems just right.
E. Volunteers (or everyone) read their sentences and the class discusses them. Some questions might be:
   1. How is the change clearer?
   2. What was wrong with the sentence?
   3. Why did you change it the way you did?
F. A new "dilly" is written on the board, and the process is repeated.

Variations

A. Have students bring in samples of "dilly" sentences.
B. The instructor brings in "dilly" sentences written by professionals —or by the instructor him- or herself! (Or from college memos, etc.)

Sample Dilly Sentences

We collected the following sentences from student writing and have used them for "dilly day" exercises.

1. I dared to touch him in risking the loss of a hand and with the passing of days I succeeded in taming this tiny life which projected so much anger and fear.
2. The deep feeling of laughter has beauty by the joy of someone or me with the pleasure of a loud, joyous laugh, ringing through the channels of the mind.
3. Days would pass, living only for her son.
4. We had packed our clothes and things we were to take on the trip the night before.
5. I kept asking him did he want to go back and see his uncle, still half-laughing, but he didn't.
6. Howard came over and stood by me and he turned me to him and he just stood there and looked at me.

4. Transcription: Teaching Punctuation, Structure, and Form

Group size: Entire class.
Time required: One class period of forty-five to fifty minutes; longer sessions can easily be used.
Materials: One tape recorder and a cassette.

Goals

A. To build self-confidence and assurance of students who have experienced little success in English.
B. To have students identify their own strengths and weaknesses in punctuation and paragraph structure.
C. To show students the multiple possibilities of form.
D. To encourage students to experiment by deliberately varying sentence structure.

Process

A. The instructor selects two or three short to medium-length paragraphs from a newspaper story, short story, manual, or text. The paragraphs should be at the appropriate reading level for most of the class and also be interesting to the students. The instructor either records or has someone else record these paragraphs.
B. The instructor opens the class by playing the taped paragraphs. They should be no longer than two or three minutes.
C. The instructor explains what a transcription is and tells the students that they will be expected to copy, word for word, the material recorded on the tape.
D. After the groans from the students subside, the instructor plays several opening words, then stops, goes back to the beginning, and starts again, giving time for students to copy the words on paper. The instructor can copy along with the students to get a "feel" for how long it takes.
E. The entire three-minute recording is transcribed by each student. Some students will need to go slower than others. Students who finish early can look their papers over; the instructor can ask these students to attempt to write several "correct" versions.
F. After each student is finished with the transcription, the instructor should give several minutes to allow students to "make

Strategy four was contributed by Jim Merlihan, Community College of Baltimore, Harbor Campus, Baltimore, Maryland.

sense" of their sentence structure and punctuation decisions.

G. The instructor should call for volunteers to put their transcriptions on the board.

H. The instructor asks the rest of the class to read carefully what is being put on the board and to compare their own transcription with those on the board.

I. The instructor explains that students are learning a necessary skill and asks the class to correct the versions on the board. The instructor might choose to designate a spokesperson for the class to go to the board and make corrections according to the directions being given by the whole class.

J. How much can be accomplished in each class will depend on the size of the class and the instructor's style. This procedure can be repeated at intervals; thus it would be best to start off with relatively short paragraphs so that students can complete the exercise in one class meeting.

K. The instructor asks students to keep a record of the kinds of mistakes likely to be committed.

L. This exercise can provide a solid base for introducing the concepts of paragraph and sentence structure, as well as for introducing writing conventions.

Variations

A. This exercise can be used to identify problem areas in an individual's writing; it can also be used to identify those writers who do *not* need extensive editing and proofreading work. Thus it can be useful in placing students at an appropriate level from the outset.

B. Have students tape-record each other and write a transcript in the same class session.

C. The instructor can be the center of attention or not, as desired. It is possible to leave a class with the problem of coming up with at least four (or as many as the instructor wishes) accurate versions of the same paragraph. The instructor should make sure that there are in fact a number of different ways that the punctuation can be marked off in the sentences.

5. Where Do I Put These Caps?

Group size: Small groups of four to six students. The instructor can group students according to capitalization problems in their writing, or students can form groups in any manner they choose.
Time required: Approximately one hour—ten minutes at the end of one class period for the instructor to explain the exercise and fifty minutes of the following class period for students to learn capitalization conventions by the peer-teaching method.
Materials: Copies of a text in which all capital letters have been changed to lower case letters. (A sample is included at the end of this strategy.)

Goals

A. To help students learn the conventions of capitalization.
B. To encourage peer teaching.
C. To dispel the myth that the English instructor is the sole source of knowledge of language conventions.

Process

A. The instructor explains the goals of the exercise, divides the class into small groups, and distributes copies of the exercise to students.
B. As a home assignment, students are told to place capitals in the text wherever they are required and to be prepared to explain the reason for the convention.
C. While completing the assignment outside of class, students may use any resources available to them, including the writing lab, an English handbook, the instructor, or other instructors.
D. During the next class period, the instructor distributes copies of the same text with correct capitalization and asks members of each group to check each other's papers.
E. After the "correction" has been completed, group members return papers to the owners and take turns explaining any errors which have been noted on the papers. The instructor may serve as a resource person in case any questions arise.
F. To check retention, the instructor may ask students to complete another exercise in class, and, if needed, the peer-teaching process can be repeated.

Variations

A. This exercise can be used to help students learn any of the
   conventions associated with the written mode, such as spelling,
   abbreviations, numbers, or use of italics.
B. This exercise can be used solely as a homework activity. The first
   three steps of the process would remain the same, but as the next
   homework assignment, students would exchange papers and
   mark corrections.

Sample Essay

All capital letters have been deleted from the following essay, which
was written by Monte Weade, a student at D.S. Lancaster Community
College, Clifton Forge, Virginia.

anglers' dismay

an eight-mile section of the james river, known as the springwood area, has been called an "anglers paradise" by many sports
writers and fishing experts. many species of fish are abundant
here, many of them of record breaking size. but for all this,
springwood remains an isolated area which is visited by very few
fishermen.

there are many reasons why fishermen from outside this
region stay clear of this section of the james. being a native of this
area, i can understand why this taboo has been placed on the
river.

the shore line on both sides of the river is covered with heavy
brush in most parts. to get to the few clear spots along the banks
requires a very strenuous hike of several miles. fishermen must
also be careful not to trespass on private property. some of the
farmers who own river frontage do not allow outsiders to cross or
use their property. the landowners have put this restriction on
the fishermen due to the carelessness of a few.

the angler who chooses to take to the river in a boat is faced
with a challenge just as great as the angler on the shore. the
irregular depths of the river, which range from two feet to an
estimated eighty feet, cause changing currents which can be very
tricky. two rapids divide the section into thirds, known as the
lower, middle, and upper sections. the upper rapids are especially dangerous to boat traffic. a fisherman may never get a
chance to fish the upper section from a boat, for there isn't any
place to launch a boat above the rapids and only a few skilled
boatsmen can reach it from the middle section.

the last and biggest reason sportsmen do not fish this section
is pollution. the jackson and cowpasture rivers merge at iron
gate, virginia, to form the james. the cowpasture is one of the few
unpolluted rivers left in virginia whereas the jackson is one of the

most heavily polluted. westvaco, in covington, virginia, is the main contributor of pollution in the jackson. the effects of the industrial waste are still very evident at the springwood section some forty miles away. the water looks as if it is almost black, and a white foam is visible on the surface very often. when certain weather conditions exist, a very foul odor is evident.

although the reasons for the lack of interest in this section are very evident, i believe there could be a vast recreational future in this section. if stronger pollution regulations were enforced and individual landowners would clear the river frontage, sportsmen would begin to take a second look, much to the advantage of all concerned.

6. Learning Punctuation Conventions

Group size: Either large or small groups.
Time required: One to three hours, depending on the number of conventions the instructor wants students to learn and the writing sophistication of the students.
Materials: Copies of an essay in which most (or all) punctuation marks have been removed. (A sample is included at the end of this strategy.)

Goals

A. To encourage students to learn the conventions of punctuation.
B. To encourage students to find alternate sources of authority for writing conventions.
C. To encourage student interaction and peer learning.

Process

A. Like the preceding strategy, this exercise is based on the belief that one really learns something when he or she has to teach it; thus, the peer-teaching basis for the exercise. For this exercise, the instructor hands out copies of an essay without punctuation (or with only one type of punctuation missing) at the end of a class period and asks students to punctuate it as a home assignment. They are to be prepared to explain the reason for each mark.
B. While completing the assignment, students may use any resource available to them: an English handbook, the instructor, the institution's writing lab, other instructors, and so on.
C. At the beginning of the class when the assignment is due, the instructor hands out copies of the same essay with all punctuation restored and divides students into groups of four to six.
D. The students exchange papers and correct each other's papers, marking only those areas which were incorrectly punctuated.
E. Students in the group "peer-teach" the conventions for those members who used punctuation marks incorrectly. The instructor may serve as a resource person, should any questions arise. (This step of the process, of course, can consume a good deal of time; part of the peer teaching could be done outside of class—in the writing lab, for example.)

F. The instructor can distribute another essay, with the same type of punctuation missing, to check mastery of punctuation conventions, and the process can be repeated, if needed.

Variations

A. The instructor can form groups based on students' punctuation in their own writing. One good approach is to group two or three students who use a punctuation mark correctly with two or three who do not.
B. This exercise can be done as an individual assignment, but besides placing punctuation in the essay, the student must also give a *written* explanation for each punctuation mark. The instructor collects these papers and assigns students to learn the convention for marks they have misused. The student must then "teach" this rule to other students during a later class period.

Sample Essay

The following essay, from which all punctuation has been removed, was written by Minnie Singer, a student at the Community College of Baltimore, Harbor Campus, Baltimore, Maryland.

Not All Women Want to Be Liberated

As a child I was taught that a woman should stay at home with her children and a man should work for a living When I was in junior high the girls took home economics and the boys took shop because these were the things that would be most useful when we graduated Of course some girls would work in office jobs even though they were married but they still had to know how to cook and sew

I married when I was eighteen and felt quite ready to play the housewife and mother Ten years and four children later I was bored with Mrs. Prim-and-proper and decided to go to work I had learned that women were *not* restricted to housework and office jobs Bunnie a friend from the local womens group suggested painting might be a good place to start After all she said how hard is it to put paint on a wall

Mr Clark the business agent for Painters Local Number 1 thought it was hilarious when I showed up at the hall to ask for work but after several arguments and a month of regular attendance at apprentice classes he enrolled me officially in the program I went to class for three months before I got a job

The first morning I reported for work at seven in what I thought was full dress union-made whites The foreman told me I had two days to get a pair of steel-toed boots This is a hardhat job he muttered chewing on his cigar In the beginning I didn't notice all the white pants hanging on nails but as more painters came in I saw that I was the only one wearing a uniform and realized they were waiting for me to leave so they could change I turned to go when Gary the foreman bellowed O.K. men time for work Gopher youd better take orders for coffee break now There's a carry-out on the corner He was talking to me I wanted to shove the cigar down his throat but the guys all started talking at once

Im Bill Coffee black

Im Ted Coffee cream and sugar

Dont forget my change

I tried to remember all the orders as I waited for my days assignment from Gary He told me to work with Frank the shop steward on the eighth floor I heard him chuckle as I walked away and then he yelled Oh by the way our elevator is out of order When I got to the eighth floor panting like a puppy I could see there would be no sympathy from my fellow workers

By coffee break I was tired and dirty from climbing over a heat duct with the rolls of plastic used to protect it from the paint I was cold because the building had no heat yet And I was desperately in need of a rest room because there were no johns for women Once we finished taping every heat duct on the site I thought things would get better At least I wouldnt have to climb so much but instead the work got harder

Ten weeks of toting five-gallon cans of paint and paste and dragging seventy-five-pound rolls of vinyl up and down through eight dirty drafty damp floors in the middle of winter made me wonder why I had ever been so dumb Then I knew how hard it was to put paint on a wall I was ready to be a housewife again

Appendix A: Setting Priorities for Diagnosing Student Writing

For more semesters than we would care to admit, we have carelessly approached the teaching of composition in our classrooms. We would assign essays from a text, discuss them in class, vaguely pointing out a few structural or rhetorical concerns, and then require students to write essays of their own. We "corrected" them all in the same manner—often ruthlessly—and graded them according to some ideal essay which was permanently fixed in our mind's eye. While the grading part of this process was partly based on rhetorical concerns, the "correction" part was overly concerned with surface correctness—the proofreading part of the writing process. Surely our students must have understood from our red marks and comments that spelling was more important than structure, mechanics more important than unity and coherence. Metaphorically, we were teaching our students to trim the windowsills before they had adequately constructed their houses.

Since that time, we have become more systematic in diagnosing writing problems. Instead of marking every writing transgression in a student paper, we attempt to diagnose, on a priority system, the *major* problem of that writing and ignore all others. When a student no longer shows that problem in his or her writing, we then focus on the next priority for our diagnosis. This is not a new approach, we know, but we think it is important for writing instructors to establish their own priorities for helping students to write better and to guard against slipping back into the questionable method of correcting everything and accomplishing little. We constantly have to remind ourselves to comment about the *good* things in a paper, to diagnose the remaining major problems, and to begin working on those problems in a systematic manner with each student, without comparing one student's writing to another.

Our priorities are set up on a simple basis: the writing problems which seem to harm a paper the most—the global concerns—are the first priority, and every other problem is ranked according to how much it tends to diminish the value or worth of the writing. A lack of structural unity, for example, is a much greater problem than a few subject-verb agreement problems or several spelling errors. Here is a list of our priorities:

I. Global concerns
   A. Rhetorical concerns
      1. Unity: logical development and flow of thought
      2. Focus: staying on the topic without wandering
      3. Coherence: "sticking together" of major parts of writing, use of transitions
      4. Pointedness: responding pertinently to the writing topic
      5. Sufficiency: saying enough to get the job done
      6. Value: the quality of thought

B. Rhetorical structure
    1. Introduction
    2. Body
    3. Conclusion
II. Other structural concerns
    A. Paragraph structure
        1. Development: "backing up" of generalizations by using details, examples, illustrations, comparisons, and so on
        2. Coherence: one sentence "fitting" with or leading into another; using transition words or phrases
    B. Sentence style and structure
        1. Sentence fragments
        2. Run-on sentences
        3. Awkward sentences
        4. Wordy sentences
        5. Choppy sentences
        6. Illogical sentences
        7. Lack of sentence variety
III. Writing errors
    A. Subject-verb agreement
    B. Verb tense consistency
    C. Pronoun reference and case
    D. Internal punctuation
    E. Capitalization (for beginning of sentences only)
IV. Mechanics
    A. Spelling
    B. Mechanics: use of apostrophes, hyphens, capitals, abbreviations, and numbers
V.   Usage questions (e.g., *hanged–hung, who–whom, can–may*)
VI. Dialect features (see Appendix B for a discussion of this priority)

We can show how this priority system works by diagnosing the following student paper.

Smiling Funeral

One of the warm summer days rather beautiful because of the clear sky. Not really a day for a funeral it seemed.

The practice of funerals being sat in a joyful maner was unusual to me. Myself being from a Western civilization were the culture is very different from that of the East and South East. The South-Eastern culture of South Korea was very old, and what I was about to take part in was only customary.

It is with much understanding that the living pass the dead on in such a joyful fram of mind and mood. For in most old cultures like that of South Korea. There is no word in the language for hell as we today know the meaning to be. The words used to express the journeys end for the living spirt of the dead is, Happy Yama. The meaning of which is simple, Over the mountain, or to ascend to a better place.

The arrangement for the funeral are set in a decorative design of bright colors and large signs. Signs proclaiming the dead persons name. Members of the procession are family, friends and guests. All of which are dressed in bright colors. Many wearing what look to be party hats. Often there are two or three drumers.

> There is a rhthemic sound and movement to the procession. Forming a dance like step of movement, steping five pases forward and two back. The casket is carried in a case ornamented with dragon heads of bright colors. From which are jung many bright colored ribbons. The case is carried on two horizontal polls which is carried by eight men. In front of the case sets the pace maker of the rhythem; also carried by the eight men.
>
> At the grave sight after the dead is placed in a round grave. There is the eating of many goods and wines. Many free spirited songs feel the air telling of love and death.
>
> The ending of the funeral is the beginning of life of the spirt of the dead. The people of the procession are left to live life pleased because the spirts of the dead is free, and has ascended. They can smile because one has gone over the mountain.

As we read this story, our red pen-bearing hand seems to have a mind of its own; it wants to underline, circle, and attack all the surface errors that this writing presents. Like Dr. Strangelove, we virtually have to struggle with our arm to keep it from moving. By our priority system, however, this is actually a relatively good writing. The author knows how to begin, develop, and conclude a narrative, he knows how to stay to the point and add sufficient detail, and he certainly has something worthwhile to say.

The important thing for us to do, it would seem, is to *encourage* him by pointing out all the good qualities of the paper. In pointing out problems, we would first go to the B section of Priority II on our list and point out sentence style and structure. Everything else, we believe, should be left alone, since marking surface errors would only tend to confuse priorities for this writer at this stage of his development. If we can keep him interested in writing, there will be time enough to work down to the lower-level priorities of agreement problems and spelling errors in his later writings. This method does not produce dramatic, overnight successes, but it does produce consistent improvement in student writing. And, in any case, it certainly beats the mindless method we formerly used.

Appendix B:
Diagnosing Dialect Features
in Student Writing

Dialect features are spoken features that regularly occur in the speech patterns of any group of speakers, thus making their linguistic system slightly different from that of another group which speaks the same language. The way a person from Boston adds an *r* to the pronunciation of the word *idea*— making it sound like *idear*—or the way a Southerner may pronounce the word *I*—making it sound like *ah*—are examples of regional dialect differences. Most dialect differences are differences in pronunciation only, but some are in word choice: a Northerner may say, "I drove my son to school today," while some Southerners say, "I carried my son to school today." Likewise, speakers from some areas of this country keep a spare tire in the *trunk* of their cars, while speakers from other areas keep it in the *boot* of their cars.

While most people are aware of and accept these regional dialect differences, they fail to recognize *social* dialect differences and thus stigmatize the dialect features of a person from another socioeconomic class within their own region. It should be understood that these features are just as regular, just as linguistically "pure," as the features of any other spoken form of the same language and are condemned only because the minority dialect users themselves are disliked, usually because of their lack of power and prestige in that society.

The black dialect (or black English) is an example of a social dialect. Although it shares most of the features of other American English dialects, there are enough variations for most Americans to distinguish a black English speaker and to condemn his or her speech as "nonstandard," "corrupt," or "uneducated." Not all black Americans use black English; indeed, many blacks who have moved into the "mainstream" of our society share the same dialect features and language attitudes of most whites. Furthermore, many of the black English features are also found as regular features in Southern dialects, which isn't surprising since most black Americans can trace their origins to the pre-Civil War South. As blacks moved to the North, they again faced social isolation—usually in urban ghettos—and their dialect patterns were retained and preserved in a new geographical area.

Most dialect features present no real problem in the written mode. Whether a speaker says '*po lice* or *po 'lice*, the spelling remains the same. Yet, many speakers of the black dialect (and of many Southern dialects) face a problem in the written mode, since their dialect features are often reflected in the written verb system—and are usually marked as incorrect verb forms.

We will not attempt to catalog the differences between black English and "standard" English here. (For those readers who are interested, we recommend Robbins Burling, *English in Black and White* [New York: Holt, Rinehart and Winston, 1973] as an excellent source on this subject.) Instead, we will attempt to point out the major black dialect features that often show up in a student's writing. Many of these black dialect verb features come from consonant cluster reduction—the tendency of virtually all American English speakers to combine and reduce a group of consonant sounds to a simpler construction. For example, most speakers would not distinguish all the consonant sounds in "I stopped to see him yesterday." For most speakers, the *ed* marker in the word *stopped* would be eliminated. Black dialect speakers simply carry this reduction tendency into more areas of their speech, leaving off the *ed* markers on many spoken verb forms, as well as on many written verb forms. It should be understood that these writers *do* understand the concept of verb tense; the tense is usually reflected in some other word or in the context of the entire speech or writing.

Compounding this writing tendency is hypercorrection. Because English teachers have intervened in a dialect writer's linguistic system in the past, that writer may be confused enough about which verb or noun to put *ed* or *s* endings on to write verbs like *beated* or *dranked* or a noun like *childrens*. Hoping to find the elusive answer to a complex, mysterious writing problem, the writer has overshot the mark in correctness, ending up with verb forms that are also marked as incorrect by the English teacher.

Dialect interference in writing, then, is not a simple thing to eradicate. It may be best for writing instructors to focus on major writing problems first, leaving dialect features as a very low priority for prescription. Once dialect speakers become fluent, sophisticated writers, they can choose whether to learn the prestige patterns. If, at that point, they choose to learn them, they probably will do so with a minimum of effort. The following are dialect features commonly found in student writing.

1. Loss of *ed* endings on past tense verb forms. Examples: "When I was a child, I walk to school every day"; "He wish me a happy birthday"; "I use to do that all the time." This loss of *ed* endings occurs because of consonant cluster reduction. In learning the "standard" form, a dialect writer often goes overboard in "correcting," e.g., "He beated the rug with a broom." This tendency is called hypercorrection and is *not* a dialect feature, but a result of a "standard" English speaker interfering in the writer's linguistic system.

2. Loss of *s* endings on third person singular, present tense verb forms and on plural nouns. Examples: "He show me his homework every day"; "I read her stories and play game with her every day." The noun and verb in the examples lose the *s* ending due to consonant cluster reduction. Again, in "correcting" the problem, the dialect writer often goes too far, ending up with a hypercorrect sentence like "The childrens were told to wash their feets every day."

3. Invariable *be* for future tense *will be*. Example: "He *be* coming in a few minutes." This construction occurs largely because of consonant cluster reduction; "He will be coming" is reduced to "He'll be coming," which is further reduced to "He be coming."

4. Double negative concord. Example: "We don't want nothing." In most dialects of English, the rule is to put negatives in the first possible position, but not on following indefinite pronouns: "We don't want anything." Other dialects—such as the black dialect—

demand that the negative go in the first possible position, *as well as* on the following indefinite pronouns: "We don't want nothing."

5. Use of *it* for *there* as expletive (filler word). Examples: "The first day at school I was afraid because *it* were only five blacks in the classroom"; "*It* was a girl on our side who couldn't hit the ball." This dialect difference is simply the result of a diction choice difference between dialects.

Authors

Carl Koch

Mr. Koch received a Doctor of Arts degree from the University of Michigan and is presently administrative assistant in charge of curriculum and faculty development at Bergan High School in Peoria, Illinois. He was previously an English teacher and department head at two Midwest high schools and an assistant professor at Christian Brothers College in Memphis, Tennessee.

James M. Brazil

Mr. Brazil received a Doctor of Arts degree from the University of Michigan. He is currently an associate professor of English and Director of the Division of Humanities, Applied Arts, Language, and Communications at the Community College of Baltimore, Harbor Campus. Mr. Brazil has held positions at several community colleges, including Jackson (Michigan) Community College, where he taught English in a special program for prison inmates.